Now That I Have Your Attention

by

Marnique Rogers

ISBN: 978-0-692-13540-2

Editors: P31 Publishing, LLC

For more information, please visit

Instagram: _marnique1

When love is incapable, and pain is perishable, hurt becomes susceptible, and unhappy fate is inevitable. Feelings convert to behaviors, and behaviors become lessons. Lessons become blessings, and my lesson was depression.

I watched my mother, who watched her mother, who watched her mother, and her mother before that. They all watched their babies get snatched. Tell me, how do you recover from that? –Marnique Rogers

Table of Contents

Chapter One Validation 1

Chapter Two Shallow 71

Chapter Three Fear 131

Chapter Four Reaction Formation 181

Chapter Five Awareness 209

Chapter Six The Ripple Effect 229

CHAPTER ONE

Validation

/vale dash(e)n/
The action of checking or proving the validity or
accuracy of something
Searching for acceptance; wilding for respect.

I asked to be accompanied by my older cousins to the Jidenna concert, but they didn't like him enough to travel out of state for a concert. That was fine. I was finally about to do myself some good and heal. I was in a place in my life where I truly wanted to be free and quite faking it until I made it. The Jidenna concert was in Columbus, Ohio where my father lived. The date of the concert was perfect because I didn't work in the summer. My plan was to get a hotel room for a night then spend the rest of the time at his house alone so I could get my thoughts together. My dad worked two jobs and was never home. He'd get about 4 hours of sleep in between the two, so I knew I would barely see him. On the way to Ohio, I saw Jidenna post on his

Instagram page that whoever he felt was 'Adaora' from one of his songs would receive a rose from him and have the pleasure of meeting him backstage. All I could think about was how amazing that experience would be. Something like that would be just what I needed to kick off this self-healing hiatus.

When I landed and got to the hotel, I decided to step out on faith a little bit. I actually prayed that I would be the 'Adaora' for that night. I had been so broken down from the previous things that transpired; I just wanted something amazing to happen, like meeting one of my favorite artists, to let me know that God hears me and that everything was going to be alright. I know you're not supposed to challenge God, but I think I prayed for something so rare to happen because I secretly didn't want to face my issues. I based the time I was going to take for myself on whether I got to meet Jidenna or not.

I got dressed early so I could be one of the first people in line, increasing my chances to be in the front. I made sure to take time to look extra enticing. When I got there, there were bout twenty people in line before me. I thought there was no chance I'd be directly in the front. When they opened the doors, everyone in front of me ran straight to the bar, and I secured my spot in the front- smack dead in the middle. As soon as he hit the stage, he noticed me and gave me a smile. That was honestly good enough for me;

my prayer and much more came to pass. I ended up meeting this girl there, which was good for me so I wouldn't be there alone. The concert was amazing; he engaged with the crowd and made us all feel like family. To my surprise, he engaged with me and the girl next to me, a lot. He even took my phone and sang one of my favorite songs, *Bambi*, on my Instagram story. When it came time to sing the song, *Adaora*, I knew for sure I was going to get the rose. He, of course, went to the other side of the stage and sung to everybody else but me. At the end of the song, he came right in front of me and handed me the rose. Before I could even get into my bag of excitement, a young girl jumped from behind me and snatched the top of my rose right out my hand. I was pissed. Thankfully, his road manager saw that he handed the rose to me. I was able to see him still. I was so elated; God answered my prayer with immediacy. It was his way of letting me know that after all the fun and games, I needed to do what I came here for.

Needless to say, my experience meeting Jidenna was awesome. When I met him, he made me feel as though we already knew each other. It was not what you'd expect meeting a celebrity. I thought when I saw him I was going to totally fan out, but his spirit was so inviting. We had small talk like old friends for a few minutes then he had to leave for the next city. I was lucky enough to get a few pictures with him too. When I sent them to my cousins, they were shocked that I actually met him and wished they would have joined me. I went to bed that night completely over the moon, and I felt more comfortable about the new journey I was on. I knew that everything was going to be alright and going to that concert and meeting one of my faves showed me that I could speak things into existence- with good intentions of course.

Before my dad went to work, he picked me up from the hotel and took me to his house. His house was very man cave-ish. After my dad left, I took a shower and got comfortable.

I brought along with me my vision board. My dad's living room was spacious enough for me to spread it across the floor and get as creative or messy as possible. I started by drawing lines, dividing the board into three sections. The first section was titled 'depression.' Under it, I wrote a couple of facts about depression—depression affects the ability to work and function, it makes non-depressed people who love you feel helpless and/or confused, and...— As I wrote down these facts, I thought about how depression affected all of my relationships- whether they were intimate or platonic. The next section was titled 'Forgiveness.' Before I could forgive I had to take myself down memory lane and allow myself to feel every emotion that came along with the trauma.

"Can you send me your kisses? I still feeeel your touch. And oooh, I need you so badly. I want you so much." That was the norm for 15-year-old me getting ready for high school, hopelessly in love with love. Waking up to Sam Cooke was equivalent to Folgers in the morning. "My days are so lonely"(The smell of the morning brew) "my nights are so blue"(The sound of the liquid entering the mug)"I'm here, and I'm longing" (cream, sugar, stir) "and I'm waiting for you" (Feeling the warmth of the concoction trickling down my throat). I was so excited for my first day that I couldn't help but to remember how tragic it was.

"STAR HURRY UP!" My mom called me about three or four times before she got irritated.

"OK mom, I'll be down in a sec!" I yelled back.

"Nowwwwww!" she demanded.

A long sigh and an eye roll later, I was down the stairs and into the car. I was ready to make my debut. I am the eldest of three girls. Mia is the middle child, and Sady is the baby. We lived with our mother and their father in a two-family home on the east side of Syracuse, New York. We were all beautiful girls. I stood about 5'2," brown skin, and shoulder-length hair, with an hourglass shape. Every teenage boy's dream, right? Wrong! Although my physical features were attractive, my personality was different...much different. I had the musical taste of an 80-year-old woman and often gazed into space imagining what life was like in the '50s. A conversation with me would always consist of how much I love the Sam Cooke, Jackie Wilson, and Frank Sinatra era. It was often viewed as strange to my peers, which is why I didn't have many friends. I didn't mind it so much in middle school, but I wanted high school to be different.

As I walked into the building, it hit me that I wasn't in middle school anymore. Five hundred kids in one building turned into five hundred kids on each floor. There was a huge foyer and long narrow hallways. It seemed like a million kids were trying to go to the same place all at once. I walked down the hall until I got to room 245- my first-period class. As I walked in, I tried to keep in mind not to come off so weird.

"Good morning class. My name is Ms. Montana. Welcome to Living Environment," the teacher said.

The classroom was arranged in a circular setting so that everyone was facing each other.

"Everyone please- take your seats," the teacher continued.

I looked around the room to try and find a familiar face.

"Every year, I do an exercise with my students to help everyone get to know each other," she said.

I didn't see anyone I knew, so I took the seat closest to the door.

"Write down on a sheet of paper your name, age, interest, and where you see yourself in five years. When we're all finished, I want you to stand up and present it to the class," she continued.

Ugh, I hated public speaking! It's not that I wasn't a people person; I just hated attention, mainly because I didn't think I was worthy. Someone always thought some part of me was weird, and it made me really shy at times.

The first couple of people went, saying the typical 'I like to watch TV and listen to music' thing and then, I heard, "Miss. Robinson."

"Oh no, it's my turn," I thought. I stood up slowly and took a deep breath. "Hi, my name is Star Robinson."

"Hi Star," the class responded.

I eased up a bit.

"I'm 15-years-old. In five years, I see myself in nursing school, and I like listening to really old music," I said.

Even though people viewed that side of me as strange, I always got excited when I talked about old music.

"What kind of old music?" Mrs. Montana asked.

"Well, I like Sam Cooke, Louis Armstrong, Jackie Wilson, Michael Jackson, the Beatles, the Turtles, the Kinks, Frank Sinatra, Stevie Wonder, Smokey Robinson, Elton John...," I responded.

"Lame," someone shouted.

I was interrupted by a cough and a cruel remark. The rest of the class started laughing. I felt like I wanted to die. I mean, I liked other music; hell, I was absolutely obsessed with Beyonce. But, for some reason I always wanted people to remember me by the things that make me different. I wanted them to remember me as the girl with the old soul. At this point, my eyes were looking at my toes. I couldn't face my classmates.

"Quiet down! Please continue Miss Robinson," said Mrs. Montana.

"Shopping and makeup," I said quickly and made it back in my seat in the blink of an eye. For the rest of the period, I stared off into space, tuning everyone out, imagining a world where I could do no wrong. That day, I entered every room with my head down and kept to myself. That moment ruined what I thought would be the best day ever. It felt like the day would never end. I just wanted to go home and sulk in embarrassment.

As soon as I saw my mother, she asked, "How was school?"

I didn't want to talk about it, so I lied.

"It was good," I said.

I kept it short and sweet with my mother most of the time. Lately, we couldn't have a decent conversation without an argument.

"Ok! Well, it's your turn to do the dishes. Make sure you do that before you do anything else," she said.

She couldn't help herself; she ended every conversation with a demand.

Surprisingly, in a weird way, doing the dishes was calming. It gave me a chance to think. All I could think about now was what happened earlier in Living Environment. My idea of high school was what I saw on TV, and I didn't want to be known as the weird, socially awkward girl.

My sister interrupted my thoughts, "Hurry up Ta Ta! *Pretty Little Liars* is about to come on."

"Ok hold on. I'm almost done with the dishes," I said.

I quickly snapped out of it and joined my sisters in the living room to watch our favorite TV show. I adored my little sisters and would do anything for them. I especially treasured our quality time. I needed it the most today, but it was short lived.

"Where's your mother!" My step-dad busted into the house in a drunken rage.

"There goes our night," my sisters and I said in unison.

"I called you three fucking times, and you ignored me. You're a fucking slut! What were you doing?" he asked, yelling at my mom.

"What the fuck are you talking about? I've been here all day with the kids!" my mother yelled.

"So, where is your phone?" he inquired.

"I don't know- probably in my room," mom replied.

"So, you ignored me on purpose?" he asked.

I hated when he started drinking. I'd been dealing with this since I was three. We counted the times he was sober instead of when he was drunk.

"Let's just all go in my room and watch TV," I said to my sisters.

My mom had been with my stepfather for thirteen years, and it had been the same routine. He would come home drunk, find the smallest thing to argue with my mom about, then go to sleep in the midst of talking shit, only to wake up and forget everything he said or that any of it ever even happened. Some nights he would bicker and break things all night until the next day. She would go to work tired, and we would go to school tired. It made us distant towards him, me and Mia, anyway. He was more like a man just living in our house with us. We had no connection with him. Our baby sister always forgave him, though. The only time she was upset with him was when he got loud when he and our mother argued. Every time they argued, I always was so tempted to jump in and defend my mother. No matter what we went through or how I felt about her, you had one time to violate her and I was on that ass like white on rice.

Before my baby sister was born, it was almost impossible for me to keep my mouth shut. What made me stop was the realization that my words couldn't stop anything. My mother was going to be with him and deal with whatever he brought along with him until she was tired. That, and she would constantly tell me to stay in a child's place. In a way it made me resent her. "Like, how can you be mad at me for defending you?" I'd ask. Her response would be that I'll understand when I'm older.

The older I got, the more I kept my mouth closed and my sisters out of the way.

"Why won't she just leave him?" Mia asked as we all walked into my room.

"I wish I could answer that for you. It makes me so mad that she just lets him come home drunk, acting and talking to her the way he do," I said in frustration.

"Is mommy gonna be ok?" Sady said.

"Yea, she'll be ok. We just gotta pray for her," I said.

"I hate him so much," Mia cried.

As much as I felt the same, that was still her dad, and hate was a strong word.

"Don't say that Mia. We gotta pray for him too," I said.

I closed my door and turned the TV on and turned the volume up loud enough to drown out the sound of them arguing. My room was medium-sized, and my queen-sized bed took up most of the room. I had a small walk-in closet with mirrors on the doors, a fluffy pink rug, and stuffed monkey animals covered my bed. Five steps to the left was my dresser that held my TV and cd/radio player and all my old-lady albums. Michael Jackson, Sam Cooke, and Motown posters were my wallpaper. We all gathered on the bed sitting Indian-style.

"How do you pray?" Sady said.

I was taught the Lord's Prayer when I was four years old, at my cousin's daycare. By six, I was able to recite the whole thing without any flaws. Every kid in the joint knew the Lord's prayer if they went to her daycare. She didn't play. It was her and my two grandmothers that instilled the love of God in me at a young age, and it never left. They didn't do it in a forceful way where we had to go to church every Sunday, but as I grew older and watched them confide in God in good and bad situations, and how a prayer filled them up with instant joy, I wanted that same connection.

"C'mon, I'll teach you how to pray, just repeat after me, you too Mia," I said.

"Our father, who art in heaven, hallowed be thy name, thy kingdom come, thy will be done, on earth, as it is in heaven, give us this day our daily bread and forgive us of our trespasses as we forgive those who trespass against us, lead us not into temptation..." we began.

Little baby Sady repeated every word correctly until we got to that part.

She said, "Lead us not into the Temptations."

Mia and I busted out laughing. As much as I played their music around the house, I couldn't blame her for thinking that's what I said. That moment filled me and my sisters with joy.

From that day on, helping people feel good during bad situations became my scapegoat. In the midst of a storm, I was able to make someone else smile and feel like everything was going to be ok. I secretly wished I could get my peers to feel me on that level. I was so proud that I had done something right by God and taught my sisters how to pray and to have a relationship with him. It made me sad that people weren't accepting of that part of me.

We ended up spending the night in my room that night, which made me happier than they knew. I was so scared of the dark. It's funny to think that my fifteen-year-old self couldn't get over that fear. The good thing about growing up in a big family was that at Grandma's house you always had a sleeping partner because of one of your cousins. The other good thing was because of the closeness in age. At some point in time, you might end up going to school with one of them.

The next day at school, I ran into one of my many over-protective male cousins, Sean. People often mistook him for a little white boy at first glance and wondered how in the hell we were related, but Sean was hardcore. There were literally no rules when it came to fighting, and he didn't play the talking game when it came to his family.

Two years prior, I was in the hallway at my middle school standing with a group of girls, and this kid ran super-fast past me, cuffing a chunk of my butt along the way. Sean was a looker, so girls always tried to find some excuse to talk to him. With that in mind, I didn't have to wonder how word got back to him that someone touched my butt. By the time lunch period rolled around, a crowd of kids was standing around Sean, who was pinning the boy against the wall telling him that he "BETTA NOT EVAA!" Ugh, I was so embarrassed and even more angry that a girl used that as a way to talk to him. Knowing how my cousin would react, that was far too small a problem to tell him.

"Ta Ta!" Sean screamed across the foyer. I was happy to see a family member. It made me feel comfortable about my high school experience. I ran up to him and gave him a tight hug.

"Hey, Sean!" I said with excitement.

He probably was the craziest cousin I had, but he was my favorite.

"Where is your class? I'll walk you," he said.

I showed him my schedule, and we proceeded to walk down the hallway. Almost every female shot me a look of jealousy or curiosity because they didn't know my affiliation with Sean. That day, Sean met up with me after every class and walked me to the next. The only moments I had alone were going to the bathroom and lunch because we didn't have the same lunch period.

I caught up with some familiar faces from middle school and figured I'd eat lunch with them.

As I made my way to the lunch line, a girl walked straight up to me and said, "You like Sean or something, because he's my boyfriend?"

The boldness and seriousness on her face made me laugh. She stared at me with confusion. I'm sure laughter wasn't the response she expected. She walked up prepared for war.

After about thirty seconds of laughing, I finally answered, "Girl, bye! That's my cousin!"

"Oh! Well, hey! My name is Bella. You probably think I'm crazy," she said.

I laughed at how she went from frantic to calm in a matter of seconds.

"No, I don't think you're crazy; it just looks to me that you don't play about your man," I said.

"Girl, you just don't know how many bitches try me," she said.

"I can only imagine. Earlier today when he was walking me to class I got the stare of death from just about every female in the hallway," I said.

"Who? Where they at?" she asked, laughing.

I couldn't stop laughing. Sean was nice looking and all, but I was impressed by his current girlfriend. He usually didn't pick the prettiest flower out of the bunch. This one looked like a black china doll. She was so pretty, and her confidence intensified her beauty. She was flamboyant. I aspired to be as flamboyant as she was one day.

"You can sit with me if you want," she said.

I didn't see any of the other girls I intended on sitting with, so me and Bella ate lunch together. She was well-liked, but she was different, the type of different I can identify with. She loved God, and we both shared a love for old TV shows like *I Love Lucy* and *Golden Girls*; we both also adored Beyonce. Her room was covered with posters of Marilyn Monroe and Audrey Hepburn. The first time we hung out outside of school, we watched *Breakfast at Tiffany's*. I was so happy that I found a friend who didn't find the things that were unique about me weird and I could identify with her on so many levels.

We also shared a similar flaw, the need to be validated. We both wanted validation from our mothers and peers. See, I wanted my peers to see and accept how special, how soulful, intellectual, and inspirational I can be. For some reason, I felt that the approval of my peers would validate that. On the flip side, somewhere down the line, my mother stopped being my superhero and I just wanted her to be that again. Bella on the other hand, for the most part, was sure of herself as far as what she wanted to be, where she wanted to go, and how she was going to get there; she was good at not taking "no" as an answer. When her peers and family didn't acknowledge that, it put her in a place where she felt she had to prove herself. She needed constant reassurance that she was 'the shit' like she said she was.

Me and Bella's friendship grew stronger and stronger over the months because we were validation for each other. We became prayer sisters. Jealousy was foreign between us, and we'd always lift each other up with the words and wisdom of God. I didn't feel so bad not having lots of friends in high school anymore. I mainly rolled with Bella during the first year of high school. She was a senior, and I was a freshman, so I knew pretty soon my go-to wouldn't be around to accompany me in high school anymore. She was set to attend a prestigious school in the fall that was miles away from home.

Then that's when I met *him*, Dame Samuel. I knew who he was, but this was the first time I had the pleasure. We shared a mutual guy friend, Garvy, and every time he came around, I couldn't take my eyes off his smooth caramel skin, tightly curled hair, and deep dimpled smile. It was the end of the year, and Bella was over the high school scene, so for the last few days, she didn't come to school. So, I met up with

Garvy often. This time, he brought *him* to our spot in the library. He introduced us, but for the first thirty- minutes we didn't say anything to each other; we just stared. Dame finally asked me why he never saw me around.

"I be around," I said back in my best flirty voice.

"Nah, I would've remembered you,'" he said. It was a task trying to hold back a grin.

"Nah Dame, chill," Garvy interrupted, "she a good girl, and don't you have a situation?"

That was the red flag for me. I wasn't interested in any *situations*.

"I'm not in that situation anymore," Dame snapped back.

The conversation started to get uncomfortable. I was mad at myself for getting as excited as I did inside when he asked why he never saw me. Dame was the type of guy who could get along with anybody. He wasn't exactly laid back, but he wasn't into any of that 'I wanna be a gangster' stuff like most guys at my school were. It was refreshing. On top of that, he was hilarious. I quickly cut my losses and snapped out of the longing dream I had of Dame becoming my high school sweetheart. Like most girls my age, when I saw a cute guy, and we flirted a little bit, I started planning my wedding day. Ever since I saw the *Temptations* scene when Otis walked behind Josephine singing to her trying to get her attention, I died for a high school relationship turned marriage by the time I was eighteen, one where we'd tell the story to our grandkids one day.

Later on in the day, Dame caught up with me, gave me his number, and said he didn't have a situation. He just wanted to be my friend. I knew what 'just wanting to be my friend' meant, but I couldn't say I didn't light up inside. I'd been eyeing him for a while now. Although Garvy looked out by mentioning Dame had a *situation*, I couldn't stop thinking about that smile. When I got home, I laid on my bed and pictured us as a couple anyway. I had to call Bella. If anybody was going to give me some solid advice, it would be her.

There were three rings, then I heard Bella say, "Heyyy!"

"Bitchhhhh, I got something to tell youuuuu!" I said, more excited than I'd been in a while.

"But wait. First of all, Bitch, where the fuck have you been? You know I need you here with me at school," I continued.

"I know girl. I'm sorry. I just can't get with that place anymore," she said, "I'm so ready to leave it's not even funny. Plus, I know it'll take one dirty look from a bitch, and I'm gonna lose my shit. I can't let bitches who don't have anything to lose get me out of character."

She was right, but I missed her. I hated having to wait to get out of school just to talk to her because a text just didn't cut it, but it didn't take much for Bella to lose her shit, so staying home was best. She'd overcome so much with personal issues and girls wanting to fight her, so I understood. Plus, I wanted her to be encouraged by positive energy as she started her new journey.

"But enough about me. What you calling me bitchhhhhing about?" she mocked.

"Ok, do you know Dame, the one who be with Garvy?" I said happily.

"Yea, I know him. Why?" she asked.

"Welllll, today at the library, he was smiling in my face talking about why he ain't never see me around," I said.

That was girl code for I think he likes me.

"Awww shit!" Bella said.

By now, she knew me well enough to know I was thinking wedding bells just from a conversation with my crush.

"You've been looking at his little ass for a while," she said.

I laughed so hard.

"Bitch, like Sean ain't little," I said.

"Don't be talking about my man," she said.

"Anywayyzzzzz," I said, "Garvy was trying to give me a heads up, on the low, saying that Dame has a situation. Does he have a girlfriend?"

"Girl, Garvy ass like you his damn self, but Dame used to be with this one girl. I haven't seen them together in a while though, so I don't think so," she said.

"Ugh, what should I do," I asked, "he gave me his number, but he talking about he just want to be friends."

"Girl, you already know what men mean when they say that," she said, "just be his 'friend' then and see where it goes. That can't hurt."

We went on to talk about her and Sean's crazy love, and I hung up the phone with hope.

"What if he's my Otis?" I thought.

Overwhelmed with excitement, I had to call my middle school best friend, Daisy. I missed her and wanted to know how the rival high school was treating her. During the times I did speak to her throughout freshman year, she had already been to multiple college parties and picked up a habit of smoking weed and drinking regularly. I was still very much a prude when it came to smoking and drinking and especially prude when it came to boys. All I knew, was I wanted to be in love one day. I wanted to feel like a Sam Cooke song.

"Bestfrannnnnn," she answered the phone right away.

"Hey, gurlllll!" I replied in my fake country voice.

"What's going on? How have you been?" she asked.

"I'm too hype. You know the boy I was telling you about, the one I was crushing on?" I replied

"Yea, you got that number didn't you," she asked.

It never took her too long to figure out what my phone calls were about. She could tell by the setup.

"Yuuummpppp," I said in my ghetto girl voice.

"Okay, okay! That's my best friendddddddd," she said.

Every time we talked on the phone, it was like having a party. We could never talk on the phone like civilized human beings. Our conversations rarely had depth to them like when me and Bella talked, but I liked it like that. Every now and again, I didn't want to be so serious and in my feelings. Meaningless conversations are sometimes needed to ease the pressure of daily stress.

"So, what's been going on Daze," I asked.

"Well, it's kind of funny that you called me first because I had something to tell you too," she said.

Now I had to brace myself; so far, I'd only heard the craziest stories from Daisy and her high school experience.

"I go out with someone from your school," she said.

"What," I shouted, "who, how did you meet him?"

"Well, his name is Rell, and I met him at a party over the weekend. You need to spend the night so you can come with me to parties over the summer," she said.

"Yes, because you seem to be having the time of your life. I don't know a Rell though. What does he look like?" I said.

"You'll meet him," she said, "he's a senior though, so you probably don't know who he is."

"Oh, my best fri-" I caught myself; Daisy was extremely jealous.

"My friend Bella is a senior, she might know him," I continued.

She went on to tell me how she only hung out with older girls and maybe two or three other girls our age. I told her how I met Bella and how close we grew over the year. She said she heard of Bella and got kind of jealous at how close she and I got. I had to reassure her that she would always be my number one chick, but it was nice to have someone I can relate to being at a new school and all. I think she was really upset that Bella and Sean were dating. Daisy had a crush on him since we were in elementary school.

We hung up after thinking of a master plan for how I was going to sleep over to go to a party and talked about what I was going to wear. I didn't have anything club-like, mostly because my mother was still buying my clothes. Daisy said that the older girls she hung with either took her and the younger girls to the mall to get something to wear or would hand-them-down old dresses that they already wore, so either way, I'd be fine. I was halfway excited because I loved being spontaneous, but I wasn't too hype about wearing anyone's old dress.

Soon after, I got a text from an unknown number. It was Dame, and all he said was "Hey," but the way I smiled you would've thought he told me I was the most beautiful girl he'd ever seen. Now that I had the approval of both of my best gals, I couldn't get the thought of having my first boyfriend out of my head. We had small talk for a while; you know, the common 'hey, what you doing' text. That was honestly enough for me.

The next day at school, I ate lunch with Garvy and Dame. I was so nervous being around him, mainly because he texted me the night before. So, to spark the conversation, I brought up that Daisy started dating someone from our school, and I wanted to know what he looked like. Garvy and Dame said Rell was their boy, and Garvy knew who she was because he dated someone from their school too. How ironic. I was low-key hyped because it started to feel like a start of a family affair.

"I go to summer school every year there just to be with her during the summer," Garvy said.

"You so stupid," I laughed.

"Dead-ass! Summer school be fun as fuck. You should go," Garvy continued.

Honestly, that didn't sound like such a bad idea. I wanted to be back with my best friend so bad, and it would be easier for me to meet her friends and hang out with them during the summer.

"I go up there too, just because," Dame added.

Now I really wanted to go. My freshman year hadn't been the best, but it sounded like summer was going to be one to remember. Now, I just had to get my mom to be onboard, and I was all set.

Bella was like the big sister I always wanted. It didn't take long for our families to put the stamp of approval on us both. My mom never liked my friends, but she knew Bella was levelheaded, and I wouldn't get into too much trouble hanging with her. Plus, she was Sean's girl, so she was family. To the public, we called each other cousins, but to each other we were sisters.

It was almost time for Bella to go to prom, and I went with her to go pick out jewelry. Bella could drive, so we went on this journey ourselves.

"You know, you're really like a little sister to me," Bella said, "I see so much potential in you, and you're very mature for your age, and I didn't expect that."

I was so happy to hear that because I felt the same.

"I get that a lot you know, about me being mature and all. I think maybe it's because I'm the oldest of three girls, and in certain situations I've encountered, I kind of had to be there for them," I said.

I got a little emotional thinking about how many times me and my sisters would gravitate towards my bedroom because of all the arguing and fighting that was constantly going on and the times I had to be strong for them. Bella knew I had a "crazy-ass step-dad" as I would put it, but she didn't really know the details. Every time she would ask, I would say something all nonchalant like, "Everything is okay."

I instantly felt uneasy whenever the spotlight was on me about touchy situations. I just dealt with them myself in the most honest way possible; I didn't want to let anyone in. I always just put it on the back burner so I could be that positive person in someone's life. I was that person for Bella. That made me feel validated. Someone who I looked up to came to me for advice. I felt like if it looked like I couldn't handle something, then she wouldn't confide in me.

"So, how's everything with that?" she said.

"I just wish my mom would wake up. It's not like this is new. This has literally been going on my whole life. I just don't know what she sees in him," I said.

"That's not normal Star," Bella said.

"I know. I don't know why she deals with it," I replied.

"I don't mean her. Let me rephrase that," she said, "it isn't that common for someone to stay with a person causing so much stress in their life. That's just a reflection of her insecurities. It is not normal for you to have to counsel yourself and your sisters through a situation that don't have anything to do with you."

"Well if I don't, we won't be ok," I said.

"It's not your job to carry someone else's weight," she said, "that's a form of post-traumatic stress." I listened as she continued, "That's the problem me and my mother have. She has all these high expectations of me. She doesn't even notice my achievement. I got accepted into one of the most prestigious schools, and you would think she would be proud of me, but no, it's just expected. Instead, she's worried about whether I've done the dishes, or if her house is clean, or am I being a role model to my siblings. It drives me crazy."

Completely ignoring the part about me, I said, "She'll appreciate you and finally see how valuable you are to your family once you leave for school. Sometimes it takes for us not to have something anymore to appreciate it and see its value finally."

"Yea, you're right; that's why I really can't wait until I leave," she said.

I rolled my eyes. She laughed. Bella knew I didn't want her to leave.

"Well until then, let's focus on making sure this prom is slayed, Hun-T," shesaid. That was pretty much the dynamics of me and Bella's conversations and friendship.

Malcolm X once said, "To beat your enemy, you have to study him." My enemy was pain, so in addition to praying and meditating, I studied philosophy. In Hellenistic philosophy, the path of happiness for humans is found in accepting a moment as it presents itself by not allowing ourselves to be controlled by our desire for pleasure or our fear of pain. We do this by using our minds to understand the world around us and to do our part in nature's plan by working together and treating others in a fair and just manner. I knew if I was put in a position to talk about anything that made me feel pain I would be stuck in a depressed state, therefore allowing pain to control me. I understood that I couldn't control most of the things that made me sad per someone else's actions, so I buried it and decided to be that positive person for other people because I knew what it felt like to not have that. Being stoic was my way to escape pain. I worked hard to be a person who could endure pain or hardship without showing feelings or complaining. I realized later that being stoic was the very thing that kept me from properly healing. I normalized hardship. I expected pain.

I convinced my mom that going to summer school even when I didn't have to would not only give me something to do besides laying around every day, but that it wouldn't hurt to keep learning throughout the summer so I wouldn't forget any curriculum. It's so funny. I didn't know how I came up with that, but it worked.

The only thing I paid attention to in the class was the clock because I was so excited about after school. When the final bell rang, I linked up with Garvy, Dame, and Daisy. We all walked to a nearby park together, and I sat on the swing.

"So, who tryna roll up?" Garvy asked.

In unison, Daisy and Dame said, "Meeeee."

I was the only one with the look of confusion, wondering what Garvy meant by, "rolling up." Garvy pulled out two Dutch Masters and a bag of weed.

"Let's roll up two and keep them in rotation," he said, "it's four heads on this, and I want to actually get high."

"Wait, four heads? I think you mean three. I'm not smoking," I said.

"C'mon stop being a lame; smoking isn't even bad like everyone is saying it is," Daisy said, "look, you like Bob Marley, right?"

"Yea, so?" I said.

"Well, he smokes!" she continued.

"He smokes for religious reasons, that don't have anything to do with me," I said.

"Well, it also doesn't make him a bad person, does it?" she asked.

"I'm not necessarily implying that it's bad. I'm just scared of being addicted to something," I said.

I started to realize I was being a Debby Downer by the look on everybody's face. I certainly didn't want Dame to think I was being a goody-two-shoes.

"I'll take one puff, but that's it," I said.

Garvy and Daisy rolled their eyes.

"I never met anyone who got addicted to weed; it's not like heroin or crack. Weed actually helps me stay calm and turn all my bad days into good days," Daisy said.

I laughed at how much of a hippie Daisy was.

"Plus, God put this here for you and me," Garvy said, imitating Smokey from *Friday*.

By the time we were halfway done with the first dutch, I completely became a part of the rotation.

"Talking all that shit, and you want us to keep passing it to you," Daisy said.

I busted out laughing. For some reason, everything became extra funny to me.

"So Garvy, when do I get to meet the lucky lady?" I asked, referring to his girlfriend.

"I'm texting her now. I told her to walk over here," he said.

"Who's your girlfriend?" Daisy said.

"I go with Kyra," Garvy replied.

Like most girl best friends, me and Daisy had a code. We knew what looks and certain hand gestures meant. It was like a secret girl language. Daisy somehow made her way behind Garvy and gave me a weird look-that was code for, "that bitch ain't right."

"Oh, I didn't know you guys were dating," Daisy said as if she approved. I had to know the details of Daisy's look, so I texted her. I was trying not to be too obvious.

Who is Kyra

Daisy must have started texting as soon as she got my message. *She a ho.' Every day at lunch she's sitting on a different nigga lap, she's known for taking people's man.*

I could hardly believe what I was reading. *whatttttttt, I should tell Garvy*

Daisy had no mercy for Garvy. *Nope don't tell his ass shit. I asked who his girlfriend was for a reason, he's also been talking to my friend Katie.*

I was shocked. *Oh lord, I can't with these niggas smh.*

After a short pause, Daisy texted me back. *Right he's gonna find out soon though.*

As obvious as I didn't want the texts between me and Daisy to be, Garvy and Dame caught on by the way our phones vibrated, almost in sync, followed by our giggles. On top of that, we both checked out of the conversation the four of us as a group was having.

"Don't be talking shit," Garvy said.

"Booooooyyy! Ain't nobody talking about you. So, BYE," Daisy said.

Me and her both laughed at how obvious it was. But, before he could really get in our asses about his girl, she had walked up.

"Hey everybody," Kyra said.

"Hey," me, Daisy, and Dame said altogether.

All I could think about was the nerve of this bitch playing my friend, looking the way she looked. I mean, I was never the one to judge, but I wasn't a fan of sneaky people either. Thankfully, shortly after, I got to meet Daisy's friends. They were nice, and ironically, they weren't the biggest fans of Kyra's either. Apparently, she slept with one of their men too.

We all ditched Garvy, Dame included, to roam the streets nearby. I had so much fun, and they kept saying how they wanted me to come to their school. I even talked about the weird shit, like how much I loved old music, studied philosophy, and something about becoming one with nature. I don't know if they thought I became a philosopher because I was high or if they just really didn't give a fuck about what I was talking about and thought I was cool anyway. That made me want to come to this school even more, especially because Bella was leaving. I felt validated in this group. They liked to listen to me talk.

Me and Dame finally got some alone time as we made it back around to the park.

"You're not like other girls," he said.

I was halfway nervous because this could either go left or right.

"Yea, well you're not the first to tell me that," I said with an attitude.

He laughed.

"It's not bad. I like it. Most girls your age worry about partying, being around boys and getting high. Give you the mic, you start talking about philosophy. That's dope," he said.

I smiled on the inside. I liked that he liked what was different about me.

"Yea, well I'm not that different. I want to be more social. 1 like going to parties and stuff, and I ended up liking weed. The only time I open up and be myself is when I see that someone likes something that I like or they're doing something I want to do. I get that not everyone is going to like the things that I like or even understand why I'm into the things that I'm into, so it's easier for me to adapt to the things they like," I said.

"But that's not being yourself. Why is it so important to you to be liked? Other than Garvy, I don't be around a lot of people because of the same reasons," he said.

"It's not so much that I want to be liked," I said, "sometimes I feel like if everyone around me finds what I'm into weird, then how can I expect to make a difference one day?"

"Well, I think you're special, and I don't think you need anyone to tell you that. I hope you just know that," he said.

I liked the way Dame talked to me. I liked that I could be myself around him.

Garvy wasn't too much feeling the same way. I ditched him as my male best friend and replaced him with Dame. I explained to him that it was different because *I liked him liked* him, and was hoping that one day I'd be more than just a friend.

That summer was exactly what I hoped it would be. Daisy and Dame lived in the same neighborhood, so I was able to see both of my two, favorite people at that time. Bella headed for her new life shortly after she graduated, but I kept in contact with her. She wasn't too much feeling the fact that I was going to all these college parties, but she understood that it was probably the most alive I felt in my life. I also met Dame's mother, sister, grandmother, and brothers. Although we hadn't made it official, I certainly was happy how things were turning out. They all liked me. Come to find out, my mother grew up with his family, and our grandmothers were friends in high school.

Dame's stepfather had a connection with some people for the state fair, and they agreed to let me, Dame, and his sister work for them, *under the table*. My mom thought it was a good idea because that meant she didn't have to help me with school clothes. We were all excited until we found out that we would be working 16 -hour days from 8 am to 12 pm, open and close, for a whole month. The work was easy though; all we had to do was strap the kids in the ride, push a button, then let them off. Me and Dame's sister, Nia, became really close during these days.

One of the good things about working at the fair was that we could get on the rides for free. So, every morning we would be the first to get on the rides as a safety test, and at night we would break at the same time and ride the rides together. One night, Nia's boyfriend came to the fair, so me, her, and Dame took our breaks at the same time and rode all the rides together. I got on the Ferris wheel with Dame, and we started talking. I suddenly felt the warmth of his hand levitating above my hand. Seconds later, we started intertwining our fingers between one another. My heart was beating fast. Then, he slowly began to move closer and closer towards me. Next thing you know, our lips touched. We kissed for so long that I swear we must've stayed on that ride for about 3 or 4 rounds.

"You know you mine now, right?" he said.

"You were mine the first day I saw you," I replied.

The best part about me and Nia becoming close was that I could tell my mom I was sleeping over at her house. That night, I slept in Dame's bed, and he held me all night. I was over the moon.

Working that summer was probably one of the most exciting things in my life. I finally had work experience, and it motivated me to keep earning my own money, but because it was done illegally, I ended up with nothing. Well not actually nothing, but in the end, I only ended up with $300 for working 16 hours a day for one month. My mother was pissed. Not pissed enough, because though I was working for someone who broke all sorts of child labor laws, she still asked me for money.

"This is all the money I have, and I have to get everything for myself," I said.

"When I was young I had to give a piece of everything I earned to my mother and Aunt Betty," she snapped.

Aunt Betty was the lady who taught me how to pray when I was younger at her daycare. Before and after my mother got pregnant with me, my mom lived with Aunt Betty.

"But mom, this is probably the only money I'll have until Christmas," I said, "you already said that because I had this job you weren't gonna get me anything for school, and it's my sophomore year. I really want to look nice."

She became angrier, "I swear! You're so selfish, and you try to walk around here like you're so Godly. You will probably get something from your dad and grandma, but you wanna be selfish. One day you're gonna see."

I stormed off to my room in disgust. Earlier that evening, I overheard her and my step-dad arguing over how he ran her gas out and how he had no money to fill her tank back up. On top of that, it was time to restock on groceries, and she didn't get paid until the end of that week. I tried so hard to follow that 'honor thy mother and father' rule, but most of our disagreements were over things that didn't have anything to do with me, and I would fly off the handle. I called Dame.

"Hey lady," he said, all sweet-like.

"Hey," I replied in a hard, irritated tone.

"Wussup? What's the matter with you?" he asked.

"It's my fucking mother," I yelled, "remember how I was telling you about how we just can't hold a decent conversation?"

"Yea, did you guys argue?" he asked.

"Not a full-on argument, it was more of the principle that fucked me up!" I exclaimed.

"Ok- slow down and start from the beginning," Dame said.

I liked that he was patient with me, and he seemed to care about what was going on with me really. Since he came into my life, I felt like I finally felt comfortable enough to vent to somebody.

"Well, you know how we only got $300 for our pay from the fair, right," I asked.

"Right," he said.

"Well, she very clearly explained to me that she wasn't getting me anything as far as school clothes in the beginning because I was already going to have money. I was fine with that. That meant more for my sisters or more money in her pocket. Now, she says I have to give her some of my money and that I'm selfish if I don't because my dad may be getting me something," I explained.

"Well maybe she thought she was going to have more than she anticipated, and she's ashamed that she has to ask," Dame replied.

"That's the point. She didn't ask. She didn't even say why. She just told me I had to give it to her and if I don't, I'm selfish. Then she threw God in my face to try and make me feel guilty. That's not right!" I said.

"Well, that's what I mean by her being ashamed. At the end of the day, you know you're going to be good as far as getting what you need, and I'm sure it's not easy that she has to ask you for the little that you do have. So, just bear with her," he said.

"I swear Dame! I don't want to fight with her, but the lack of respect or appreciation is what gets me mad. I wouldn't have a problem giving her anything if it was explained to me like that. Ugh, I don't know. I'm just really upset at how hard I worked, and I have to give it up," I said.

"Sadly babe, that's going to be the case more than once in life, and sadly, mothers don't feel like they need to show respect or appreciation," he responded.

After we hung up, I just laid there on my bed, staring. I started feeling like I was a horrible person for reacting the way I did. I never wanted to be the disrespectful child, and selfishness wasn't a part of my character. So, despite my personal feelings, I gave my mother $100 that day. I was the only child of my father's, so I did know that he would help out. I reasoned that I reacted that way because I had underlying feelings about the way she handled things with my step-dad.

My sophomore year wasn't too different from freshman year as far as me being antisocial. I was satisfied with the fact that I made new friends during the summer. Daisy and I were closer than ever, I had Dame and Garvy here, and me and Bella kept in contact on the regular. I ended up reconnecting with an old associate from middle school, and I made friends with one of Dame's female friends. They became friends through his ex, so I had to play her close.

Rule number one: never trust a female around your man.

She became someone I confided in. I took advantage of the fact that she knew Dame really well, and I wanted her to be comfortable with telling me specific things about Dame. We had some things in common like the fact that we can get really deep. It seemed like she'd been through more things than a woman twice her age. She just didn't know what to do with her feelings, so there I was again, making sure day in and day out that somebody else was ok.

My sixteenth birthday rolled around, and to say the least, it was one of the most special birthdays I ever had. My mom got me a cake designed like a record player, and the record that was playing was The Jackson Five's *Sixteen Candles.* Dame had bought me a whole plethora of CDs from a store called Sound Garden. You could literally find anything from the 30s to the 2000s- DVDs and CDs. Of course, he got me what I liked, Sam Cooke, Frank Sinatra, Jackie Wilson, the Beatles, and the Temptations, two of each, along with Victoria's Secret underwear and a gift card to their spinoff store, PINK. I wanted to give him the moon and the stars that day.

I hadn't seen Bella since Christmas break, and even that wasn't enough to catch her up on all the things that had been transpiring, but I had to call her on the spot to tell her what I got for my birthday. Only she would understand how special that was to me.

"I think I'm ready to, ya know," I whispered to Bella as I snuck into my room.

"Ready for what, Bitch?" Bella said all intense-like.

"I want him to be my first. I never felt like that ever in my life, and well, I am sixteen," I said.

"OH, EMMM GEE, not my little Ta Ta," she said.

I laughed. "It might sound a little weird, but I just want to able to give him something more."

"I know damn well you're not talking about a baby, Bitch," she said.

"Fuck no," I laughed, "I honestly feel like having sex with him will bring us closer. I really feel like I want to be with him forever."

"OMG, you're in love! Just be careful and remember to always stay in control; call me and let me know how it goes," she said.

I had no idea what to expect or when I actually wanted this to take place. I never really thought about sex or had that feeling for anyone and honestly never thought I would. Well, like always, I had to confirm my decision-making with BOTH of my female best friends, so I called Daisy.

"Hey, Daze," I said.

"Happy birthday bitch," she answered.

"So, let me just jump right in. I think I want Dame to be my first," I said.

"Oooooooooo shitttttttttttttt! Yes, do it. I think you should. I fucks with Dame!" Daisy yelled.

I already knew what to expect from Daisy. I just wanted to increase the confidence to let Dame know I was ready.

I went back into the kitchen where my mom, sisters, and Dame were. I tried to think of what I wanted to say to Dame along the way. I motioned for him to come into the living room so we could talk in private.

"What's up baby girl," he said.

"Well, first of all, I just wanted to say thanks for the gifts; you have no idea how much this means to me," I said.

"You're welcome. I figured they would be perfect because all your old lady-ass listens to is Sam Cooke and Frank Sinatra and whoever the hell else," he laughed, "but I didn't want to stop there. I know how much you like to look nice, and almost every time I call you when you're at the mall you're in the PINK store getting your *five for twenty-seven* panties."

"Thank you, baby. I appreciate that, and I wanted to thank you in a very special way," I said.

HIs eyebrows rose. He knew what that meant. He stepped to me a little closer.

"And what you mean by a special way?" he asked.

My prude ass was so scared that I pulled out my phone and texted him what I meant by "in a special way." He walked up and started kissing me long and slowly.

Then he whispered in my ear, "I don't think you're ready."

I got all tingly inside. That tingly feeling was deadened by the seriousness on his face.

"Wait, are you telling me that you don't want to do it?" I said with confusion.

"All I'm saying is you don't have to thank me like that," he said.

"Oh, how sweet," I said sarcastically. I could tell something was off.

"I just think you're asking me out of excitement," he said.

"What kind of shit is that?" I yelled, forgetting my mother and sisters were in the next room.

I could tell that he could tell I was thinking some negative shit by the suspicious look on my face. But, before I could get the 'are you gay' question out my mouth, he took a deep breath and said, "Listen, I'm not exactly experienced in that area."

I was surprised that he wasn't embarrassed to tell me something like that. I was happy. That meant this was something that we would be doing together.

"I didn't mean to yell," I said, "but that's what's going to make this that much more special."

"So, when do you want to? Where we gonna go?" he said.

I looked directly into his eyes as I spoke. "I don't know. All I know is I want you to be my first."

Weeks went by before we were alone again. It was a Saturday, and my mom, sisters, and their dad went to Rochester to go get my step-sister. I had the house to myself, so I invited Dame over. Today was going to be the day that we really got to KNOW each other. I was nervous. When he first came over, we did the usual. We watched a movie, snuggled, and made out. Most people call what we did *Netflix- and chill.* We started off inches apart, which quickly turned into centimeters. I turned on one of my favorite Jackie Wilson songs to set the mood, more so for me than him. I sat back on the couch, and as Jackie Wilson started to sing, I got into the groove with the song.

I took a deep breath as he slowly started to kiss my neck. Jackie continued singing in the background.

The kisses transferred from my neck to my chest, up my shirt to my belly. Then, he paused. He pulled down my pants, then my panties.

"At lastttttttt," I thought.

Just when I thought I was about to lose my innocence, a memory reminded me that my innocence had been long gone. It sent me into a post-traumatic shock.

They teach you in kindergarten not to trust a stranger. In about second grade, they tell you not to trust the guy in the white van with candy. What about the family member who passes out dreams? I remember being as young as six or seven. My mom worked two jobs, so Mia and I spent a lot of time at our grandmother's house. My aunt, her children, and my Uncle Norm lived there as well. Uncle Norm was the fun uncle. He resided in the attic. Up there, he had a whole studio setup, complete with a mike and a homemade recording booth. He was really talented at making beats. My sister, cousins, and I spent most of our time up there writing raps and making songs. My uncle would let us record them on Christmas and Thanksgiving, or any other family gathering, for that matter. I didn't have much life experience to write anything meaningful, but I knew the concept of a catchy hook, thanks to Cash Money Records.

So, that was my job. My uncle told me my hooks were legendary, and he could get me some kind of record deal. He told me that one day I could be famous enough to write a hook for the late, great Michael Jackson. He told us all that if we worked hard enough, he can make sure we would all be in the spotlight someday.

Cousin Betty lived across the street, and she ran her daycare out of her home. She had young children our age, so we put them on to Uncle Norm's plans. I was passionate about making hooks. Every day after school, I would run upstairs to the attic to show Uncle Norm what I cooked up. Then one day, he told me I could be more than just a hook writer. He popped in a cassette tape.

"This is a young rapper named Trina," he said, "you remind me of her. The way you can make up a hook, the way you speak, the way you're shaped."

"I don't think I ever heard of Trina before," I responded.

He pulled out a KING magazine, and she was on the cover. A snake tattoo covered her back, and she had a body chain wrapped around her. The caption read, "Trina, the baddest bitch."

"She's pretty," I said.

"You can be just like her," he said, "listen to how she raps. You can start making raps just like that. You can be a model just like she is, and you have a way better body than she does."

He went on, and on, and on.

"This is what a model is," I said, "she don't have any clothes on."

"Models model their bodies. Have you ever heard of your body being a work of art?" he said.

"No," I said shyly. He then showed me a picture of a bust of David and his naked body then said, "See, art."

"Ok," I said, "but first I want to practice rapping like Trina."

"Well, I don't think you can be as skilled as she is right away. But you have the body and the face to be a model now," he said.

"But, I don't know anything about modeling," I said.

"I can help you practice, and plus, the lady told me she needs someone by the end of this week, and I told her you'd be the best person for this; think of it as an art project," he said.

"I'm kind of nervous. Maybe Ashley or Nisha can do it," I said.

"NO!" he yelled. "I thought you wanted to be famous one day, and to really be successful you have to be able to do more than one thing, and never tell anybody your plans because they will be jealous."

I did want to be famous, and if my body is art, I reasoned the art project wouldn't be so bad.

"Ok, I can try," I said.

"Ok good," he said, "I have some videos you can watch, but first go downstairs in my room and look through all the magazines that look like this."

He pointed to the KING magazine. "Pick the picture you want to do, and we can start practicing," he continued, "but remember, don't tell anybody what you're doing, alright?"

On the way down to his room, I kept telling myself not to be nervous and that this was going to make me famous; this was going to validate me.

"When I'm famous, I can meet Michael Jackson, Janet Jackson, and the whole Motown," I thought.

These thoughts made me excited for this "art project." I skimmed through the magazines and found a picture of Mya I really liked. She had on what looked to be pink shorts with a matching pink top that showed little to no belly. I was about to run back upstairs to show Uncle Norm the picture I found, but my mom was there to come get me.

The next day, I showed him the picture of Mya.

"No, TA TA," he said, "it has to be one of Trina. The goal is to be like her, right? Mya don't write raps. I'll just pick the picture for you."

He picked the picture of Trina with no top and a black bathing suit bottom on. I didn't really like how exposed it was but kept convincing myself that it was art. He popped in porn and told me that it would help with how I should pose.

"Even though the goal was to be like Trina, you always should be original and make something your own," he said.

I was uncomfortable. The only body part I ever saw was my own. These ladies were more full-bodied, hairy, and would do things to each other that I never knew could be done.

"Ok," I said, "I think I know which one I want to do."

I said that so I wouldn't have to watch anymore.

"Maybe you and Ashley can try one after you do yours. Let's practice," he said.

Dame was about to put the head in, and I panicked.

"NO, NO, NO, NO! Don't touch me!" I cried.

"What the fuck? What's the matter?" he said.

"I just. I don't want to do it. I don't want to do it! I don't want to be touched!" I was crying hysterically.

"C'mon. We can do it together. I got you, babe," Dame said.

"No Dame, I really don't want to do this." I said.

"All that shit you was talking. I knew you were a fronter! You're still a little-ass girl!" he yelled.

"Get the fuck out my house!" I went from scared to angry in a matter of seconds.

"Little ass girl?" I hit him. "You're the one who tried to swindle me with all that 'no babe, I don't think you're ready. I never done this before' bullshit! GET THE FUCK OUT MY HOUSE NOW!" I pointed to the door.

As we walked out, I slammed it behind him, and I ran up to my room. Thoughts of Uncle Norm surfaced again. I never told anybody about him, and I didn't feel like filling anybody in today, so I got on my knees and prayed. I tried to remember how I got through this as a kid. I got into a chakra position, held up the sign of expression, then of survival and began to meditate. After that, I laid down and imagined a life of a peaceful childhood. I imagined things with me and Dame going well and as planned. I stayed in my bed and listened to Elton John's whole album. I had *Bennie and the* Jets on repeat. I never quite understood what that song actually meant. But that song symbolized the complexity of my being, of my thoughts. It calmed me. It uplifted my spirits. It was a song about nothing.

The first person I called about anything was Bella. This time I called Dame's female friend.

"Hey Ta, what's up," she said.

"Hey, girl. I got a question?" I said.

"What's up?" she asked.

"So, I decided that I wanted Dame to be my first," I said.

"Omg, really?" she said.

"Really. He said it would be special being that it was BOTH of our first time," I said.

She laughed, "Both? Don't say anything to him Ta Ta, but that's the same thing he told my cousin, and now that you say that, I don't know when the nigga first gave it up."

"Girl, we was about to, but then I didn't feel right, so I said I didn't want to do it anymore. He got mad and called himself cursing me out. I screamed at him and kicked him out," I said.

"Omg, for real? Are you guys still together?" she asked.

"Girl, I don't know, and I'm not really sure if I give a fuck. Honestly, I just want to relax for the rest of the weekend. I'm stressed," I said.

"I feel you girl. You know you can always come to my house, and we can roll something up," she said.

"That actually sounds like a plan. Let me get dressed and come over," I responded.

After we hung up, I went down the roster and called Bella and Daisy. Bella was proud that I stuck up for myself and didn't want me back with his ass. Daisy laughed her ass off when I told her how I hit him and told him to get the fuck out.

I walked to Shay's house because it was only a hop skip and a jump from mine. On the way, I contemplated on whether I should call Garvy or not and tell him about his boy. I knew the conversation would've turned into how he told me not to fuck with him in the first place, so I canceled that before it even started.

Shay's slick ass met me at the door with a blunt and Dame.

"Girl, I ain't come over here for no extra shit," I said, turning back around and proceeding to walk back home.

"Wait!" Dame said.

"Boy, bye!" I yelled.

He said, "I didn't mean to spazz like that. I just really wanted it."

I was mad as fuck that he yelled those words so loud. So, to save myself from any further embarrassment, I sped- walked back to him to talk.

"What the fuck is the matter with you screaming that shit?" I said, "and Shay, you know you dead ass wrong."

"Sorry girl. He called me right after you did. I can't say no to my brother," she said.

I rolled my eyes.

"Let's talk," Dame said.

"Fuck out of here. I'm a little-ass girl remember?" I said, pushing past him to go back into Shay's house. He pulled my arm back.

"Look, you bugged the fuck out back there, and you were so ready before. What's going on? Talk to me," he said.

I took a deep breath. I never told anyone about Uncle Norm, but I knew that if I expected anything to go further with Dame, and for him to not think I was a complete weirdo, I had to tell him.

"Look, Dame. It's a really long story, and honestly, this ain't the place for me to be telling you, so I guess you're gonna have to wait," I said.

He walked ahead of me and told Shay thanks for the bud and that WE were leaving.

We got back to my place, and I started talking. He was silent the whole time, and I showed no emotion. I re-lived it once that day, and I gave myself time to grieve it, and I really didn't want anyone consoling me on this matter. I then explained to him the only reason I told him and to just leave it as that. He didn't have any words for me anyway. The last thing he said before he left was that he felt like a complete asshole for reacting the way he did.

Contrary to my belief, the result of sharing that information with Dame was that things became distant between him and I. Coming over every day after school turned into me seeing him only on the weekends. When asked, he blamed it on the fact that he was a senior and was focusing on graduating, so I didn't question it. I often turned to Shay for advice to see if she could give me some inside information on what was going on with him, but that was useless. Her loyalty was with him. I believe that people are reflections of their environments. One of Plato's theories of form questions the "father-son" relationship and its influence on how the son treats people, women in particular. Dame's parents weren't together, and though he adored his father, he had a lot of resentment towards him after many years of broken promises. I noticed because of that, he would isolate himself. I figured that the correlation between disappointment and isolation was Dame's way of coping, a coping method I too had adopted. I was smart enough to know that his isolation was because he was disappointed that we hadn't had sex and was trying to wrap his head around the bomb I had dropped. So, I didn't question his absence. I just gave him space.

But, something was different. He and Shay had been spending time together after school, and he would say that he was smoking with her to relieve some stress. Then, Shay would rock me to sleep with her bullshit analogies and would say because they've been friends for years he felt more comfortable venting to her and that soon he'd come around. It didn't sit with me too well. I was about to go out of town to visit my father and his father's side of the family and thought I'd use that time to clear my head and think of my next approach.

I didn't really like going to visit that side of the family. It was different. They were passively judgmental in the name of Jesus. Like my mom's side, my dad's side of the family was raised in the church. They believed if Jesus couldn't fix it no one could, and if you don't live a certain way you won't be accepted by Christ. I knew otherwise. I lived otherwise, so I could never be any part of myself around them, and I felt uncomfortable.

My father was always in between relationships, so I would never stay at his house when I went to visit that side. I would stay with my cousin, her husband, and their kids. We would wake up every day at a certain time, eat at a certain time, do an activity at a certain time, and go to bed at a certain time. It used to make me feel like the way I lived at home wasn't the right way, until I got older and was able to differentiate between real and fake. They didn't associate with any other family members if their mom didn't. That meant my great aunt (their mom) and everyone who came from her, her brothers, my father, and me. That's because my great aunt and grandmother were best friends. I went there toward the end of the school year because we had a family reunion. In the south, they got out of school earlier than we did. I planned on being around my father and grandfather that whole weekend. They were the only two who weren't on a high horse, and they conversed with EVERYONE in our family.

To my disappointment, I still had to stay with my cousins. I kept in contact with my squad the whole time, and Dame said he wanted to talk to me when I got back. Between not knowing what we were going to talk about and keeping up with the facade of this family, I was stressed. I had none of my CDs. I didn't feel comfortable meditating in front of them, and I never had the privacy to pray how I wanted to pray. The relationship I had with God at this point in my life had graduated from me knowing who he was to actually being intimate with him. So, when I prayed, I came to his throne bold, honest, and seeking refuge just as he wanted me to. I preferred doing it in privacy so my conversation with him could be as real and raw as possible. My grandmother taught me that a relationship with God is like a parent and child relationship. Just as I come to my mother or father for understanding, possessions, and comfort, that's how you come to God, exactly how you would to your parents. That way, he would know that you depend on him.

A long seven days later, I came back to my hometown anxious to make things right with Dame and anxious for the summer to start. Me, Shay, and the other girls I connected with kept in contact while I was away, so I had some type of peace of mind that at least I'd still have my girls. On top of that, Bella was back in town for the summer, and I was dying to know about the college life.

That morning, I took my time getting dressed. I had gotten my hair done the previous day, so I had a fresh wrap. I mastered the art of the middle part with my natural hair long before it was a thing. I put on the leggings from *PINK* that made my butt look extra big, a matching fitted shirt and these cute sandals I got from *forever 21*. I was only allowed to wear mascara and eyeliner as far as makeup went, and I took my time doing my mascara, as one of Daisy's friends showed me. I outlined my entire eye with the eyeliner. It was simple and cute, but you couldn't tell me shit.

Me and Dame had plans on skipping that day to chill in the library to talk. For mediation purposes, I asked for Garvy and Shay to be there too. Since it was the last week of school, nobody cared about going to class, or school for that matter, unless they were trying to make up some school work. I walked into the building, and Garvy met me at the door. We walked up to the library, and he bought us a cup of coffee. Dame met us in the back at a table that was secluded from other parts of the library. Shay couldn't make it because she was one of the people who didn't do shit the whole school year and tried to make everything up last minute.

The first thing that came out of Dame's mouth was, "I'm sorry."

"Sorry for what Dame?" I said back sarcastically.

"Sorry that I've been so distant; I just needed some time to think about what I really wanted," he said.

"What do you mean by that? Were you thinking about breaking up with me?" I said aggressively.

"Listen, babe," he started.

I laughed. "Now, it's 'listen babe.' No, listen Dame. I'm not with all that extra shit. If you don't want to be here, that's all you have to say."

"Chill Ta," Garvy said. It was evident that I was pissed the fuck off.

"When you told me what you told me, it threw me off, and I needed some time to figure out if I wanted to deal with someone who had so much baggage," Dame said.

I rolled my eyes.

"But I know that you're a good girl, and I probably won't ever find that again. You're special, and I know I don't want another nigga making you smile but me. I don't want another female holding me down but you," he continued.

"Here's the thing Dame," I said, "I thought I made it very comfortable for you to come and talk to me about anything, especially because I shared something so personal with you. Right then and there is when you could've been like whoa, I don't think I can deal with no shit like that."

He cut me off and said, "But I love you!"

Garvy choked on his coffee. I was shook.

"I just want to do better and be better for you if you let me," Dame said.

There was an awkward silence, and then I said, "I love you too."

Garvy looked stunned as he watched those words stumble out my mouth. He looked at me like he wanted to tell me something.

We walked out of the library together hand and hand, and I saw my friend walking towards us with Dame's ex-girlfriend. When Dame noticed them, he let go of my hand. I've been in contact with my friend when I was away and expected to link up with her, so I walked up to her and said, "Hey."

As I walked up, Dame's ex-girlfriend screamed, "OH really, Dame? Fuck No!"

Then, she smashed me in my face. It caught me so damn off guard, and I started spazzing and swinging in every damn direction. Garvy scooped me up so fast and carried me down the stairs and out the door. Dame grabbed his ex, and my so-called friend stood there laughing.

"Let me the fuck go Garvy!" I yelled.

"Hell no, Ta! You do not need to be fighting over that nigga," Garvy said.

"Where he at? What the fuck is that bitch problem? And let me the fuck go!" I screamed.

Shay ran outside to see why Garvy had me pinned up in the air in a ford nelson.

"What the fuck is going on?" she said.

"That bitch Ashley put her hands on me!" I screamed, not giving a fuck if that was her cousin or not.

"What? When? Why? How?" Shay asked.

"That's what I'm trying to figure out, so if you don't mind

finding your brother so he can explain all this shit, that'll be great," I said.

She went inside the building to go find him.

"If I put you down, you have to promise to be calm and just take a walk with me," Garvy said.

"Ok, I'm cool. I promise," I said.

He let me down. The first thing I did was give Bella a call. Bella called my mom, and they both were on their way to get me. I was hot, and since Garvy wouldn't let me fight her, I needed to get off the premises.

"So wussup," I said to Garvy in my deebo voice.

"First of all, calm that shit down with me. I'm not the one you need to be mad with," he said.

"Sorry, but I'm tight right now, she got me all the way fucked up!" I said.

"Man, she reacting off what that nigga be telling her," he said.

I stopped in the middle of my tracks.

"Which is?" I asked.

"Promise you gonna stay right next to me until your mom come," he said.

I already figured it was some fuck shit going, so I decided to play calm so I could know exactly what the fuck was going on.

"Ok. I'm cool. I promise," I said.

"The whole time you were gone, this nigga been kicking it with her, and word is he been kicking it with her throughout this whole school year," Garvy said.

My body filled up with anger. I tried to reason what would make him do me like that. All I could think of was the fact that I didn't have sex with him. I couldn't stop hyperventilating.

Garvy kept saying, "I told you! I told you!"

I didn't want to hear that shit. My mom pulled up with Bella. Bella hopped out of the car before my mom could park.

"Where the fuck she at? Matter of fact, where the fuck is his lame ass at," she asked.

I couldn't breathe. Garvy put me in the car.

"Man, I don't know where he at. I just grabbed Ta and took her down here. We ain't see him yet," he said.

I sat in the car, silent with tears rolling down my face. All I could think about was him telling me right before all this happened that he loved me. There had to be an explanation.

On our way back to my house, my mom and Bella kept asking me what happened, but the words couldn't come out of my mouth. Bella called Garvy, and he told them everything. They were pissed. Shortly after, my mom spotted Dame and a girl walking up the hill.

Bella yelled, "I know that's not them!"

Seeing him walk with her made me feel like I got hit by a car. To my surprise, my mom rolled down the window and said, "Dame, you dead-ass wrong for this shit, and don't you bring your ass back to my house, eating my food, all in my daughter's face."

Ashley got mad and yelled, "What the fuck?"

I rolled my window down and said, "Bitch, I don't know what you're 'what the fucking' about you knew what it was."

"Man, just go somewhere. Go home," Dame said. That was another blow to the chest.

When I got home, Bella sat with me in the park and just held me while I cried. I didn't have words. Every time I felt like I wanted to talk about it, I felt like I was going to throw up. I still didn't tell Bella what I told him about Uncle Norm. She still didn't know that story. I didn't want to explain that story and why I thought it had something to do with Dame's dishonesty. I felt dumb for believing Dame when he said that they were over and been over. I should've just listened to Garvy. My mom said I didn't have to go back to school until I took my regents and that she was going to switch schools because she didn't want me around that shit anymore.

For days, I didn't eat or sleep. He never called. I didn't have the energy to pray or meditate, and every old song reminded me of the love I longed for, the love I thought I had with Dame. I turned my phone off. I didn't want anyone trying to console me or tell me I was going to find better or tell me just to get over it. None of that sat well with me. None of that was gonna take this feeling away.

About three days went by, and I decided to call him. The first time, there was no answer. The second time, there was no answer. I called a third time, and there was still no answer. Finally, he picked up about the sixth or seventh time I called.

"What do you want Star?" he asked.

"What do you mean what do I want? How could you do that to me, Dame? I thought we were better than this," I said.

"Look, Man! Just go on about your life. We're over," he said.

He hung up. I couldn't breathe again. I regained strength to text him. I needed answers.

I sent him a bunch of text messages, one after the other.

Is it because we didn't have sex?

We can now if you want to.

No response. He was ignoring the hell out of me. I kept texting.

I really do love you, and I can see myself being with you forever.

Can we please just talk?

You just told me you loved me.

He finally responded, but his response was sharp, even hurtful.

LEAVE ME THE FUCK ALONE...DAMN, IT'S OVER!!!

I fell to my knees and prayed. I never felt so stupid and so low in my life. I thought I did everything right. I knew another guy would never understand me the way he did. He wanted to learn from me. He taught me a lot. We learned together. He thought the things that most people found weird about me special. He knew I was rare. How could I live without my validation.

The outward appearance is a manner of presence. No outward appearance is without light. There is no light and no brightness without the opening. Even darkness needs it. How else can we happen into darkness and wander through it?

- Plato

CHAPTER TWO

Shallow

shal low SHalo/
Of little depth

Plato once said the platonic idealist is the man by nature so wedded to perfection that he sees in everything, not the reality, but the faultless ideal which the reality misses and suggests. After the break up with Dame, I became the epitome of the platonic idealist. Starting a new high school was exciting news for me. I was going to the same high school as Daisy and all the other new friends I made through her. After spending days in my room without an appetite, crying over the reality that Dame played me like a fiddle, I decided that I wasn't going to be the broken-hearted girl. I convinced myself that everything I knew about love was a lie and everything described in all those Jackie Wilson, Sam Cooke, and Frankie Lymon lyrics was just that- lyrics. I convinced myself that God had stopped listening to me. Meditation couldn't bring me back to life anymore. I was dead inside. Instead of putting any type of thought into anything, I decided to roll with the punches, fall in line and as long as I got through the day, then all was well. I was becoming shallow.

The first phone call I made when I was able to speak again was Shay. Partly because she blew my phone up the most, partly because I knew she had the answers I wanted, and partly because sympathy from Daisy and Bella would've sent me back into a deep depression.

"Oh my god girl- I was starting to get worried, I've been calling you all week," she answered.

"I haven't really been in a talking mood," I said dryly.

"Listen, girl, let me just start off and say that although Ashley and I are cousins I don't really fuck with her like that and trust me- I had no idea that they were even talking," she said.

"Mmmmm," I replied.

"I'm so serious Star- I wouldn't even do you like that. Me and you became so close, and you were always there when it came to me, and my relationship drama and I wouldn't sit back and let him play one of my best friends and my cousin," she said.

I wanted to hate her. Truthfully, the biggest part of the reason why I confided in her so much was because I knew she knew so much about Dame. After that, she became someone I confided in for more than just my issues with Dame. She also knew about my home situation and all the shit I went through there. I'm just so mad that I ignored my intuition.

"After me and him didn't have sex, he became really distant," I said.

"I'm so sorry Ta. These niggas ain't shit," she said.

I quickly changed the subject because I didn't want to fall back into depression. "Do you have any Regents to take this year?"

"Yes, I got the Global Regents," Shay said.

"Oh yeah, me too. We should meet up after, then I'll come over after school," I said.

"Ok cool," she sounded happy that I was no longer angry with her.

I stayed home every day since everything happened with me and Dame. My mom really didn't know what to say to me. She just saw the pain. Along with not eating, I didn't shower. I couldn't get out my bed. I forced myself to stay sleep because it hurt too much being awake. Today was the first day

I showered and ate. I threw on the first pair of sweatpants I saw, and my mom drove me to school in complete silence. "I'll text you when I'm done. I might go to Shay's afterward; I'll let you know," I said as I was getting out.

During the test, all I could think about was running into Dame or Ashley. Overwhelmed with that thought, I just filled in the multiple choice without reading and bullshitted my way through the short answer essays. After the day I tried talking to him, and he shot me down, I blocked his number and erased any memory of him out my phone. I didn't come to school looking my best, and I definitely didn't want either one of them seeing me looking bad. As soon as I was done, with the test I texted Shay to let her know to meet me outside by the benches they had in front of the school. Not even a minute later she was out.

"You're done already?" I asked.

"Girl yes- I ain't know that shit anyway," she said, laughing.

I cracked up laughing. "Thanks, Shay."

"For what?" she asked.

"I haven't laughed in so long," I said.

Before I could start the waterworks, she grabbed me and hugged me.

"Can we go to my house?" I asked, "I don't really wanna be away from my bed, but I would feel better if I had some company."

"Yes, I'm here for you girl," she said.

I texted my mom to come get me and to let her know that Shay was coming as well. She came and got me with my sisters in the car, and they all seemed so happy. It lightened my spirits a bit. My mom played Nicki Minaj's song Itty Bitty Piggy and all of a sudden Sady yelled, "You know I keep a bad bitch- let me sign ya boobs!" The whole car started laughing. She was only six. My mom yelled at her for cursing, but couldn't help but laugh at the fact that her little self knew the lyrics to Nicki Minaj. "That's my part," she said. The way she yelled it, I could tell she felt more liberated saying boobs and didn't realize she said a curse word. Nobody put joy in my heart like my sisters. They were still laughing when we got out of the car. "Ok, that was so long ago. Y'all still laughing?" I said.

"Look behind you," Mia said.

Just when you find the strength to be ok, life says, "Surprise!" There he was, Satan himself. Dame hopped out the back of my mother's truck. I felt so frustrated and confused. I wanted to curse my mother out so bad, but I couldn't bring myself to be that disrespectful, and for some reason, I felt like Shay knew all along. I pushed past everyone, grabbed my key and opened the door. Going to my room was too easy; it didn't have a lock, and I didn't want anybody to get to me. I went on our balcony and locked the door behind me.

My emotions were everywhere. At first, I wanted to throw up because that hurt feeling surfaced again. Then I started to get a little happy that he was here. Then I wanted to fight. I wanted to fuck his mothafucking ass up for making me feel the way I did. Ten minutes went by- then twenty, then thirty- he was still in my house. It was starting to get hot outside, and I was thirsty, so I finally unlocked the door and went inside. My mom and sisters went to their rooms, and Shay was in mine. There was no one left but Dame and me. I just sat there and looked blankly into space. It was useless to try and run. I didn't have any words for him. Maybe I had too many words for him. I didn't know where to start or how I wanted it to end.

"I'm sorry, Star," he said.

I didn't move a muscle.

"I don't even know what to say- but just hear me out," he continued.

I stared deeply into his eyes. I wanted to make him feel uncomfortable. I wanted him to see how much I was hurting.

"I did you wrong, my heart went out to play, but in the game, I lost you," he said.

I sat there trying my hardest not to flip the fuck out. No, this nigga was not reciting the lyrics from Smokey Robinson's *Ooh, Baby Baby.*

"I know I made some mistakes, but I'm only human- not everybody is perfect," he said.

"Now this nigga is playing," I thought.

He really tried to switch up the words to make them his own.

"You not serious, right?" I said smiling.

"See, I got you smiling again," he seemed excited.

I was mad at myself for giving in. "Seriously though, Dame, why are you here," I said.

"I really want to apologize for everything. I feel bad that I lead her on. Her sister reached out to me and told me how sad she's been watching us in the halls together and spending so much time together. I told her that we would always be friends, but then I started to get confused. I didn't know if I made a mistake by leaving her," he said.

"So, you're here becauseeeee," I said.

"Ta, at the end of the day you are my first love, whether we had sex or not, whether I was with someone else before you or not," he said.

"So, you lied about having sex for the first time?" I asked, completely disregarding what he said.

He paused a long awkward pause, and then said, "Yes."

"Did you have sex with her while we were together?" I asked.

"NO," he shouted.

"So, question? If you guys were 'just friends' why the hell did she feel like she could put her hands on me, and what the fuck was the whole 'leave me the fuck alone I don't want you shit' 'bout?!"

"Ta-" he started.

I cut him off.

"Do you have any fucking idea what I've been going through? Crying, stressing. I couldn't eat. I couldn't sleep. You made me feel like I was crazy, you told me literally seconds before all that shit happened that you loved me, and now here we are in my living room and you giving me some bullshit-ass story! Fuck out of here, something must've gone wrong. She probably don't want your ass anymore and now you sitting here in my face singing this song! How the fuck did you even get in contact with my mom?!" I yelled.

"She saw me walking towards your house, and I asked her for a ride. I told her how sorry I was and that I wanted to make it right with you. Babe, I really am sorry, and no, she didn't break anything off because it was nothing to begin with. I walked her home because she called my grandmother and told her some bullshit-ass story because she was in her feelings. I felt so stupid when you and your mom saw that. Her sister called my grandmother, and we ended up having a whole sit down. It was a mess. I figured you wouldn't forgive this so I told her I would work something out with her. Every day without you was the worst, and I told my grandmother that it was you who I really wanted to be with and she told me to go get you so yes, here I am asking you if we can just work on us TA- please," he pleaded.

I didn't know how to feel or what to believe. In my heart, I knew I loved him, and I knew he loved me but what he did was so cruel and unforgivable. I didn't want to be weak or vulnerable anymore. "I don't even know how I feel right now, Dame. You gotta give me some time to think about it," I said.

"That's fair," he said.

"Yup, I'll talk to you later," I said.

I got up and walked him to the door. He tried to reach in for a kiss, and I curved him. "Have a good day, Dame," I said.

"A'ight TA- you got this one," he seemed a little let down.

I tried to put together all the pieces and try to find some truth to his story. I didn't know how their relationship was, but it seemed pretty farfetched to me that her sister would go the extra mile just so they can be back together.

Dame earned his way back in- or at least he thought he did. After speaking with his grandmother and she confirmed his story, I forgave him. I was still holding on to everything that happened. People lie for their family; grandmothers too.

Social media was a big part of me not letting it go as well. Every other status that popped up on my Facebook feed was shots sent toward me by Ashley or one of her friends. Me and my cousins were like a gang, so, it was constant arguing between me, her, her friends, my cousins and anybody else who had an opinion on the matter. It made me so sick, and I got tired of telling him to check her. It made me less and less attracted to him.

To get away from all this mess I wanted to spend time with Daisy and the rest of the girls. Dame and I had been together every day since we made up. I guess it was his way of showing me that he was serious about us. But, I finally had a real social life with a group of girls and the mess with Ashley and the peanut gallery dragged on for weeks, and I needed some girl time.

Dame was supposed to come to my house today, but I really wasn't interested in being up under him, so I texted him to cancel plans.

I'm gonna spend the weekend at Daisy's, I need to get away and have some fun. This Ashley shit is stressing me out. I texted.

He was quick to respond. Why the whole weekend? I wanted you to come to my grandmother's house for dinner tomorrow.

I held firm to my plans. I'm sure we can make something happen, I just really want to have fun and let my hair down this weekend.

"T'ght! Man, my grandmother gonna be mad, but ok. He probably was shocked that I didn't give in.

Dame always tried to make me feel guilty by throwing his grandmother into the mix. I didn't give in this time- I really needed time with my girls. The entire time I was at Daisy's, Dame would text me saying how he was sad that I wasn't with him and how it's not a good look to be hanging out with my friends at parties while I have a boyfriend. So much for a stress- free weekend. We came to an agreement that we would attend parties together. It kind of annoyed me, but I just thought that's what you did in a committed relationship.

The first time we went out together was a disaster. We went to a friend's birthday party at her house. The crowd was mostly people my age and people I knew since middle school, so I was having fun mixing and mingling. Everywhere I went Dame was right behind me. Anybody I talked to Dame talked too. I got one moment alone to talk to a guy friend I hadn't spoken to in a while. His father coached Mia and my younger cousin, and he was raving about how nice Mia was in basketball.

Dame spotted me and made his way over to us. He started pinching my lower back to get my attention. At first, I thought he just wanted to ask me a question or something, so I turned around and said aggressively, "What? Can't you see I'm talking?" He looked at me like I said, "Fuck your mother!"

"Oh- you talking? You just gonna stand here and flirt in my face?" he said.

"Who's flirting? This is my friend," I said.

I didn't entertain the insinuation that I was flirting. I knew Dame was jealous and being controlling so I kept on talking to my friend, completely disregarding the fact that he clearly didn't want me talking to another guy. He stayed next to me that whole time digging in my back, and I finally turned around and screamed at him. Usually, people try to hide their crazy, but not Dame. He started screaming about how I know this boy like me and I'm being disrespectful and how I can't talk to any guys. I was so embarrassed. In the midst of Dame yelling at me, I went to find my friend to tell her that I was leaving. I called my mother to come and pick me up and started walking towards the way she was coming because I had to leave immediately. I walked three blocks, followed by Dame insulting me. I ignored him while tears rolled down my face. When I saw my mom getting closer, I took off running toward her car so he wouldn't try to get in the car with me. Knowing my mom, she would've let him in.

On the way home, I contemplated on whether I should break it off with Dame. He had become so disgustingly over-protective, and I couldn't live like this. I already had been distant because of the Ashley situation, but I stayed. I stayed because I needed to feel like I won after I went through so much embarrassment. I was hanging onto Dame like a trophy at this point. My love for him was on a downward spiral, and I realized that I was too young to be feeling like this.

Shortly after I arrived home, Dame was downstairs banging on my door. I knew that if I didn't answer he wouldn't go away and that would stir up a whole plethora of mess with my mom.

"Are you insane?!" I said while opening the door.

He grabbed my arm, pulled me in close and pointed his finger in my face. "No, are you insane?" he yelled, "don't you ever walk away from me!"

I snatched away from him and went back into my house and up the stairs. I'll be damned if I let a man put his hands on me or do anything close. I was not my mother. Right on my heels Dame came busting through my front doors like this was his house. My mom jumped up so fast off the couch- you could tell Dame forgot where he was at. He apologized to my mother and saw himself out.

He blew up my phone- text message after text message, begging me to come outside. It shocked me the way he grabbed my arm in a jealous rage like that. So, without further ado, I broke up with him via text message and blocked him from calling or texting me. Here I was yet again, sitting in my room crying over the man I thought Dame was. My mom came into my room asking me what happened, and her advice to me was that "men do crazy things for love."

"Well I don't think I want to be in love anymore," I said back to her.

Those were the ideas I was feeding myself about love. I believed if a man acts jealous, it's just because he is in love or if a man constantly wants to know your whereabouts that meant he cared. Drake taught me that jealousy was love and hate at the same time and Dame taught me that jealousy reflected insecurity. I made the decision that night to never be around anybody like that ever again.

Later that night, my mom rushed into my room telling me to put some clothes on. I was thinking one of my sisters got sick or someone in my family passed away or something. The last time my mom rushed into my room and told me to put clothes on, we found out my grandmother had died.

"What's going on?" I said.

"Dame's grandmother just called and told me that he was on the north side in the middle of the street, jumping in front of cars," she responded.

I hopped up so fast. "What," I asked, "and what are we supposed to do? Did she call the police?"

"She said she doesn't want to and the only way he will come back home is if we bring him," she said.

I often wondered why my mom did so much when it came to Dame.

On the way to wherever street he was on, I sat in the car staring blankly, imagining how things would be if I just gave it up, if I just never would've met him and listened to Garvy. I was only 16, but I'd been feeling like a 40-year-old married woman who had a delinquent son lately. I didn't want to talk to him. I couldn't believe he showed out this bad to get my attention. I had my mom call his phone to see where he was located.

If I didn't know any better, I would've mistaken him for the neighborhood crackhead, the way he was in the middle of the street, jumping out at cars, acting like he wanted to take his life. At the sight of my mother's truck, just like magic, he was happy again. He walked to my mother's car like we came to pick him up from work or something.

"Dame, are you alright?" my mom said.

"Yeah I'm good," he said, "I was just really stressed out and decided to take a walk."

My mom was so stunned at the answer that she just said, "OK," and kept on trucking.

I was pissed. The whole time, I was thinking about how insane this boy was and happy that I made the choice to break up with him.

We finally made it to Dame's grandmother's house. She was standing there, looking worried. I felt so bad. While her and my mother talked, I decided to have a serious talk with Dame.

"Listen, I don't know why you thought it was ok to not only worry your grandmother but worry my family at 3 o'clock in the morning just for attention, but this just made me not want to be with you that much more. That's so not cool Dame, and I don't know where we went wrong, but there's no trust in this relationship, and it drives me crazy that you think I'm actually out here talking or flirting with other guys. We are together all the time," I said.

But I just wanted you to talk to me," he said.

"The moment you decided to grab my arm the way you did, the conversation was over. You know better than anyone- by word of mouth and from actually seeing it- that I don't want to be in any kind of abusive relationship because of what constantly goes on in my house. So why in the hell would you think you was just gonna slide like that?" I asked.

"I'm gonna marry you one day; I'm just so scared of losing you. I see the way niggas look at you, and you just be sitting there entertaining them," he said.

I rolled my eyes. "I don't know how you think you're going to marry somebody when you clearly have trust issues, and from the looks of it, deeper ones than that. I never even gave you a reason to believe I would ever cheat on you. I'm only sixteen. I'm lucky my mom even letting me see one guy. I don't have a car. I can't go anywhere. No other guy is allowed at my house, and I definitely can't go anywhere else, so I don't even know why you acting like that." I said.

"Ever since you started hanging back out with Daisy, all you want to do is be with your friends and partying. That's not what you do when you're in a relationship," he said.

"Well that's why I don't want to be in one," I said. I felt the need to explain to him that I still had a full life to live because he obviously didn't understand. "If you think at sixteen it isn't abnormal for me to want to be with my friends, you're the issue. Then you talking about getting married? Shit, it already feels like we are. Don't you wanna hang out with your friends?" I said.

"You're different- I thought that this is what you wanted. For two years all you've been saying is how you wanted a fairytale relationship and married at eighteen, and I fucked with it because that's what I wanted too, but I guess you lied to be in a relationship!" he exclaimed.

"LIED TO BE IN A RELATIONSHIP?" I mocked, "I don't want to be in anything like that with someone who wants to be in control of my life. I guess now that it's just me and you and you have no more 'friends' and 'situations,' your true colors are starting to show."

I got out of the car. I was done with this situation and done with him. I still had the rest of the summer to enjoy.

On the ride home, my mom was telling me how his grandmother was saying they have a history of depression, and she thinks that he's depressed. "She asked me to ask you to at least be his friend," my mom said.

I replied, "I don't even know if I can be that for him right now; I have to get rid of my own depression."

"So, you want to kill yourself," my mom said.

"No, but that doesn't mean I'm not depressed," I responded.

"You're just being so selfish right now. Even after seeing that- you're so heartless," she said.

I took a deep breath; I was not in the mood to argue with two people tonight. She was one of those people who associated mental health with crazy and who believed in God, but the only scripture she knew was Psalms 23. It was hard for me to connect with her on a deeper level when it came to religion and when it came to facts. We rarely saw eye to eye, and it frustrated both of us, and that was only a small part of why we always argued.

"You just don't understand, Mom," I said.

She continued yelling, and as always when I felt sad and stuck, I started to drift off in a daydream, envisioning a life where everything was perfect.

With all the drama of Dame and my mom and step-father, I was in desperate need of a girl's day. I went almost half the summer without connecting with Bella, and that's whose advice I needed right now. I called her so we can meet up and talk before she went back to school. She told me how she fell in love with someone from our town who was not Sean and that she was strongly considering moving back here to go to school, along with other reasons. I told her about Dame and how trapped I felt. She was happy that I finally got rid of him; she never really liked him anyway. She always imagined me with someone smart and into all the spiritual stuff that I was into. She had described me as a modern-day Hippie. When I talked to Daisy, she was also happy and ready for me to come to her school so we could fuck shit up together. Honestly, my spirit was feeling very vengeful. I wanted revenge on my old self- for falling for someone like Dame, for not living my life to the fullest. For being that weird girl for so many years.

HHS was bigger. Everyone was filled with school spirit, and it seemed like almost everyone got along, and I already had a squad, so at this point everything was perfect. My first day went really well, I ended up making a new friend in almost every class, and it went perfect because they were already friends with my squad. Dame had been blowing me up the entire summer, but I was doing exactly what he wouldn't want me to do- partying, smoking, drinking, you name it. I had agreed to just be his friend, holding conversations with him here and there. It never could stay friendly because he would always try and bring us up every time we spoke. He was right outside the school door when I got out of school every day for a week to walk me home when school first started. To not cause a scene, I complied. I eventually ended up telling him that I liked someone else. Which was the truth and that he couldn't be coming up to the school walking me home every day. Of course, he got angry and went through the usual stages of when we disagreed. First, he called his grandmother; she would call my mom and my mom would try to convince me to be nice to him. But, I didn't care. I was miserable dealing with Dame. If I knew any better back then, I would've just let Ashley keep him.

I decided that if I was going to deal with anyone else it was going to be worth my time. I wanted someone on the basketball team or football team. Someone who had a job so I can go on a real date and not just to somebody's grandma house. I wanted to have all the latest styles and shoes, so that meant I had to get a job. I wanted to completely re-invent myself because the old me attracted men like Dame. That couldn't happen anymore. I was happy that I had a little crew, and that we always had fun, but now I was on some 'once you crossed me there's no second chances' shit, due to how many secrets was kept when it came to me and Dame's situation. I was all about looking good, living my best life, and being around people who felt the same.

The first thing I did to get a little closer to the athletes was join the cheerleading team. I cheered on varsity at my old high school, and the HHS coach knew who I was so I knew I was going to get a spot on varsity. Me and one of Daisy's friends, Jewel, tried out together; being that she was already a cheerleader, I felt comfortable. Daisy cheered too, but she wasn't quite varsity ready. I liked Jewel. She was tall and pretty, with long hair and her body was to die for. She called herself butterscotch thickness, and that became her nickname to the whole crew.

Every day after tryout practice, guys that used to go to the school would come up and watch the cheerleaders and football players practice. Jewel's old boyfriend and his friend came up there a lot. Jewel introduced us, and we all became friends. Jewel's old dude befriended me to get to her back, but shorty was cold-hearted. So cold-hearted. In fact, that one of her old flames took time out to write a song about just how much. I'd never met somebody who got over things as fast as she did. When she said she was done with someone- friend, lover, whoever- she meant that. During our friendship, I don't think I ever saw her stress about anything or dwell too much on a bad thought when it came to relationships. I admired that- it was something I needed to be around and something I hoped to inherit.

Halfway through the second tryout week, we decided to not go through with it. Jewel was tired of the dynamics of how the team was being ran and didn't really like the girls, and I felt the same, so we decided to just attend every football and basketball game they had with the rest of the crew. I became a social butterfly, and me and Jewel was becoming closer and closer. Three-way phone calls between me, her, and Daisy became phone calls just between her and I. I forgot about everything and everyone from my old school- including Shay. Not that I didn't like her anymore, but I was so happy with how things were going that I didn't want to hear anything about Dame and I knew she'd be the one to bring him up. My girl Bella was doing her thang in school, finishing up the year where she was and then she was coming on home to me. Until then, I knew I had a crew that was gonna hold me down for a long time.

For the most part, me and my crew had a pretty good understanding of what loyalty meant. Yes, we had outside friends, but if anybody fucked with one from the crew, they fucked with all. Whoever had a problem knew to be ready for all of us, no matter how many fights went on at home. How hard Dame tried to make me jealous. How long Bella was gone. I was good because my crew was solid. I was liked by almost every person I met. I felt valid. I could do this for my last two years of high school easily. But just when you think everything is everything, life goes, "HA! HA," like a kinder-garten kid playing a prank on one of her peers.

All of a sudden, people I spoke to every day in class started giving me funny vibes and funny looks. It didn't bother me at first because like I said I was on some "you got one time to cross me" shit. I told my crew about the funny vibes, so they wouldn't be surprised if something were to ever pop off. One night I got a phone call from Jewel's ex-boo. I already put her on D to how he would call me plotting on ways to get her back. I would even secretly put her on three-way so she could hear the shit he was saying. He would even try to set up double dates between his best friend and I. Problem was, he had a girl, so these phone calls from him was getting really old really fast. I almost didn't answer.

"Hey Juss," I said.

"Yo! I got a question," he replied.

"Oh gosh, listen- not to be rude, but Jewel is just not inter-ested anymore," I said.

"NO sis, it's not even about Jewel, well kind of," he said.

"Ok, so what's it about then?" I asked.

"I know Daisy y'all girl and everything, but she over here telling my girl word for word how I'm trying to get Jewel back," he said.

He said more, but that's all I heard before I called Jewel on the next line. It had been slight jealousy because me and jewel became so close. But, that was due to the fact that we liked to do the same things, we didn't want to party every single weekend, so the days the other girls would party, me and Jewel would be in the house eating food, smoking and watching movies or at the mall. But, never did I think anything I told her would leave her mouth. Especially to somebody we didn't even speak to.

After Juss told us the whole tea, me and Jewel spent hours on the phone putting two and two together.

"So, what we gonna do Jewel- are we gonna press her tonight or tomorrow?" I said.

"I don't even know; I'm still in shock. She be in our face, putting her two cents in just to go back and say something to this girl. I don't even want to speak to her," Jewel said.

"Let's just fall back," I said, "and if she asks why, that's when we can tell her."

I didn't really like the idea of dragging it because if I knew Daisy, she would never ask. Then again, I hated fighting with people I put my trust in. I had a pretty reckless mouth. If I weren't me, I would want to fight me. I didn't want to end a friendship that way so, falling back was the best thing for me to do.

Me and Jewel didn't see Daisy at all the next day. Before we could even put the fallback plan in motion, it seemed like Daisy was already one step ahead of us. When we did see her, she made it clear that she picked a side. She ate lunch every day with Juss' girlfriend and her crew for the rest of the school year. I didn't stress over the situation too long though. I didn't have time to keep figuring out why people couldn't be loyal. So, we walked past each other through the hallways like we weren't best friends for five years. We were in secret competition with one another. Anything she thought she did to make me and Jewel jealous, we did it bigger and better.

I had got a job at the smoothie place in the mall, and Jewel's spoiled ass got money in her account every week from her parents like a steady paycheck. For twin day she and Juss's girlfriend wore matching shirts. We cashed out. We wore everything the same- from the hairstyle to the accessories and all. We got the yearbook committee to feature us when they did the section of the yearbook's spirit week. For Daisy's birthday, they bought her a pizza; for mine and Jewel's birthday, we went all out. We decorated each other's lockers. Mine was Michael Jackson covered of course, and hers was covered in Hello Kitty. Lunchtime we bought pizza and wings for each other- a cake, balloons, gifts- and the rest of the crew screamed happy birthday when the cafeteria got quiet. Petty was my middle name; there was no sign of me slowing down or anyone slowing me down.

That was just the high school side of my life. I really liked the job I had at the mall. It was dead smack in the middle of the food court, where everyone had to pass if you came to the mall. I saw everyone. People from my old high school, family members I hadn't seen in a while, and I met lots of other people. The age group at my job was from 17 to maybe 25. That attracted so many young people bringing our clientele up tremendously. My manager was super cool; she was hardly ever there and left it up to us to run the joint. We got lots of tips that ranged from $5 to $50 a piece. It was a really sweet gig.

The staff was great. I was nervous because I didn't want to be in an uncomfortable working environment and I wasn't the biggest fan of having too many female friends. It worked but because we all had our own separate and unique roles. I was the pretty black girl with "the body"; there was the pretty Spanish "smart girl." Two lesbian lovers, the quiet weird guy who just listened to everyone's convo. The fake wannabe gangsta, and a yummalicious snack who became my next love interest. He met every expectation of my now shallow mind. He was a tall, brown skin, pretty boy. He dressed nice, had TWO jobs and was in college. I worked hard for my own, but it would be nice to have someone who had a job so I can go on a real date. I asked the Spanish girl Talia what his deal was. She told me that he was going through a break up with his high school sweetheart. Not this shit again I thought. "Oh, I'm good on the niggas and the not knowing what to do about their ex-situations," I told Talia. "I don't blame you girl she always popping up here randomly checking on him; one time she thought I was dating him- but I got a man," she said.

"And see, I don't do too well with bitches; she will get smacked," I said.

Instead of backing the fuck off, I decided to try being his "friend" first instead. My logic was, "Hey, he isn't in a relationship, and I'm only gonna be his friend."

When really, what I wanted was his attention to finesse my way into his heart. So, I put a plan in place. Every day that we worked together, I would find random things to talk to him about. I paid attention to the things he talked about with his friends when they came to the job. I knew the things he liked and disliked. I caught on to the fact that he liked basketball and who his favorite team was. Both my sisters played basketball for their school every year, so I had the advantage of learning everything there is to know about basketball and the Miami Heat.

Checkmate! I had everything down to a science, I knew how many layups, assists, passes and points the key players had in each game and why it was important. I actually started liking basketball in real life and favored my own team and players. Our conversations about basketball got more and more interesting. The more I learned, the more I understood, so I wouldn't be one of them girls who didn't know what she was talking about. I made it my business to come to work and talk to him about the game anytime the game was on. By the time the championship rolled around, he asked me if I wanted to come over his house and watch the game with him. That was one of the happiest days of my life. I wasn't just happy about the invite, I was happy because I felt in control of my life. I wanted him, I worked hard, and I got him.

Well to me, it was only upward from there. When I went on break the first person I told was Bella; she was happy because she knew that meant that I was seriously over Dame. She was excited that I was excited about someone new- because she was too. It seemed like our lives were always in sync. Whenever her life was good in a specific area, so was mine; the same if it was bad. Next person on the list that would've been called was Daisy, which explained why I slipped up and dialed her number. Just as quick as I dialed, it was as quick that I hung up. I immediately called Jewel. She knew me well enough by now to know that I was a hopeless romantic and no matter how shallow I was becoming, she knew that deep down inside I wanted to be somebody's wife. This was just a different way I was going about it.

"Girl, I need you to come to the mall asap," I pleaded.

Jewel was so spoiled it wasn't unreasonable to just tell her to stop what she was doing and come meet me somewhere with cash in hand.

"Ok- what's going on?" she asked.

"Girl, Roman asked me if I wanted to watch the championship game with him so you know I got make sure I'm looking cute," I said.

"Ok girl- I'm on my way," she said.

I also invited Talia to come along because she was cool and a shop-a-holic, which I loved. I liked the idea that I had different friends in different places for different reasons. I liked it better that way. Three's a crowd when there's a group of friends, but three can be company when you need all ya best gals to come together on account of you- and no one is forced to hang out together all the time.

His favorite team was the Miami Heat; so, I got the jersey, the hat, the socks, and the leggings that went with it all (the kind that highlighted my figure). I also got matching Mac lipstick. I was ready!

The day of the championship fell on a Saturday, which was perfect because I could stay over late. When I walked in, he had a couple of friends over. I instantly got uncomfortable because I thought this was a him and me thing.

I texted Jewel. *Girl, I'm here with him AND a bunch of other niggas …. I wanna go home lol I'm mad.*

Jewel must have been waiting with her phone in her hand. Her response was quick. *Oh, hell naw! I thought it was gonna be just you and him??????*

My fingers moved furiously across my keypad. *Me too. I'm tight. I'ma text you in like five minutes and act like you're my mom so I can go home.*

Jewel was tickled. *LMFAO! OK!*

I sat there uncomfortably for about three minutes before I picked up my phone to text Jewel the "911" text. All of a sudden one of his friends jumped up in my face and said, "Damn Roman how you get her- hey sweetie you don't want this fool do you? You need a nigga like me!" I stared at him with a facial expression mixed with surprise and disgust.

"Get out her face man- she good, she chilling," Roman said. I sat there with an awkward smile. Roman could see I was annoyed and I was contemplating on whether I should text Jewel the "911" text.

"And you fine too- Roman ain't gonna know what to do with that," another friend said.

I forced an awkward smile.

"If ya'll don't shut the fuck up and watch the damn game Man," Roman said.

I saw that he was just as annoyed as I was, so I decided to stick around after seeing him make an effort for me to be comfortable. I texted Jewel and told her that I was ok and that I would call her later to tell her everything that happened. After a while, I loosened up and joined in with the screaming and yelling. The night didn't go as planned, and whatever I thought I was gonna accomplish by it just being me and him went down the drain. His friends were shocked at how much I knew and that I wasn't just some pretty girl trying to finesse my way into their friend's heart. Little did they know that's exactly what I was trying to do, but in the midst of that, basketball found its way into my heart.

By the end of the night, his friends were my friends, and we were planning the next time we were all gonna hang out with one another. After they left and it was just Roman and me, he told me that he liked the fact that his friends thought I was cool. That made me happy. "One step closer," I thought.

"I had fun tonight- you're really a cool chick," he said.

"And you know this, Mannn," I said, trying to be cute and immediately regretting it.

He laughed. "Sorry about my friends- them niggas be wilding sometimes."

I said, "Yea it was annoying at first, but they're cool."

Shortly after his friends left, he took me home. The ride home was awkward. We didn't say anything to each other, but the music was on, and we just vibed out to Drake. Fifteen minutes later I arrived to Casa de Star, unbuckled my seatbelt, said, "thanks, had a good time, bye"-and proceeded to get out the car.

"Hey Ta," he said.

"Yea?" I replied.

"What you doing tomorrow?" he asked.

"Nothing. Why? Wussup?" I said.

"Let's go to the movies," he said.

"Ok," I said.

As soon as he pulled off, I turned the cool girl act off and went nuts. I felt like I was in a love movie as I skipped up the walkway singing Blue Moon- The Frankie Lyman version. I had all intentions of making my usual phone call rounds, but I was too over the moon for that. Bella and Jewel were gonna have to wait until tomorrow, and I'd just fill Talia in at work. It was 6:30am when I woke to hear my mom and step-dad arguing.

"I told you I'm using the money for my daughter, either that or a bill get paid pick one," my step dad said.

"You're such a liar, you're only using your daughter as an excuse," my mom said.

"Not today, Satan," I thought. Waking up to the sound of my mom and step-dad arguing was not abnormal, but it wasn't what I wanted to hear on a Sunday morning, THIS Sunday morning especially. Before I let that ruin my morning, I made a decision that no matter what, nothing was gonna ruin this day because I had a date with Roman. I put my pillow over my ears so I could drown out the sound and go to sleep. Not even a minute went by before Sady's little body crept into my bed, followed by Mia's.

"Why won't she just leave him?" Mia said, followed by a burst of tears.

"I don't know; maybe one day soon- just remember to keep praying," I said.

"I prayed last night," Sady said, "and now they're arguing today."

104

I looked both my sisters in the eyes as I tucked them in. "It doesn't work like magic. You have to pray that mommy will one day see that this isn't worth her happiness and have the courage to move on. In the meantime, we have each other to talk to. Now try and get some rest, I'll turn the TV up louder."

Though they argued the whole morning, we managed to get a few winks of sleep in. My whole life, I was always told to stay in a child's place, but I was so tempted to ask my mom 'woman to woman' why she put up with his shit. I loved my sisters, and I didn't want them growing up in an environment where they felt like they couldn't run to their mother when they needed her about men. But, no matter what came out her mouth, she was showing us that as long as you love someone, you're supposed to put up with all their shit. It made me sad that I could count the seconds after they argued and my sisters would appear in my bedroom. It hurt me that I couldn't give them a solution. One thing I knew for sure though--God was close to the brokenhearted and wounded in spirit. Prayer was always my answer.

I always believed that during the entire duration of your day, one bad thing happens, one good thing happens, and everything else is in between. I counted the argument as the "bad thing" that happened today. The rest of my day was focused on my date with Roman. As usual, when I wanted to impress, I took time deciding what I was going to wear. I decided I wanted to go for a grown and sexy look, and I recently saw an H&M ad where this lady had on a button up with jeans and heels on. So, to my best ability, I imitated that look. I had a rose-colored fitted button up, dark washed high waist skinny jeans and some black pumps. I wore my natural hair in my middle part, flat-ironed bone straight, and I did my makeup very natural and wore dark lips. All I could think about was being mature. I felt like I was pretty mature for my age, but Roman had Dame about 3 years on me. I was 17 and Roman was 22, and the last thing I wanted him to think was that I was just some little girl with a silly crush.

He picked me up at 7pm. Our movie started at 7:45. We had to walk past our job to go to the movies, and we knew everybody was gonna be talking about it. No one knew of our rendezvous except Talia. When I got in the car, he couldn't stop telling me how pretty I looked. I couldn't stop smiling... well cheesing. He looked and smelled so good I couldn't stop staring. Waves on swim, skin was glowing (which for me was a plus). He had on a button up polo shirt with a grey cardigan, dark-washed jeans, and the latest Jordans. He definitely pulled off the grown and sexy look. I was especially a sucker for his smile and how much chinker his eyes would get when he was smiling. He reminded me of the cover of Sam Cooke's Mr. Soul album.

The ride there was quiet, and the sounds of Drake filled the air. When we arrived, he was so gentleman-like. He opened my door, and we walked hand and hand inside the mall past our co-workers screaming, "Awwwww shittttt," as we went up the escalator. While he got our tickets, I thought I'd text Jewel real fast to let her know how things were going so far.

I typed quickly. Now, this is what I'm talking about. I can't wait to tell you about this date, but I'm already excited about how things are going so far.

What he got on, what he smell like? Jewel, just like Daisy, was all about what a nigga looked like or had on, especially his shoes.

He has on a polo button up, dark washed--Before I could finish the text, he grabbed my hand again and led me into the movie theatre.

We went to see Project X. The good thing about going to see a funny movie is that you can always indicate if someone is having a good time or not. I got to see a goofier side to him that he didn't really show before. I liked it. The side jokes and comments throughout the movie let me know that he felt comfortable and cared if I was comfortable as well. When the movie was over, we left all smiles going back down the escalator to our coworkers saying, "Yaaaaasssss!" Then, there it was, that chinky- eyed smile I loved. I was pretty high off life. Being the gentleman that he was, he opened the door for me to get back into his car "Dame who?" I thought.

"I had a good time," he said, "you're a pretty cool chick."

You're a pretty cool dude yourself," I shot back.

"We definitely gotta do this again," he said.

"I'd love that," I said with a smile.

I got out the car and finally looked down at my text. I had 15 text messages from Jewel saying,

Bitcchhhh! Text me back. What's going on? I can't wait.

Seeing that made me more excited about telling her. I knew I wasn't gonna be able to sleep because of the thoughts of how perfect this date was, so I had no problem staying up on the phone all night filling her in.

When I walked in, the mood was the same mood as a normal Sunday night. My two sisters and mom in the living room- one sitting down in front of her getting their hair braided, the other waiting on the couch next in line.

"How was it?" my mom said.

Although my smile was a dead giveaway, I answered, "Good," all modest, like I do this every day.

"When do we get to meet him?" she said.

"As soon as I'm sure about him. Right now, we just chilling," I said.

"I hate when young people say that- what is 'just chilling' supposed to mean?" she asked.

"Well, in more lame terms it basically means that we're just trying to get to know each other- see if something sparks," I replied.

I wasn't in the mood for 21 questions, but I still wasn't gonna' let anybody ruin my Sunday.

"Oh that's interesting," she replied.

I just rolled my eyes and went to my room. That night, I stayed up and told Jewel about my date and how I was happy to finally be completely over Dame.

The next day at school was a complete blur. In every class, in every conversation and through my free periods, all I was doing was daydreaming about my date and what my future would look like with my new boo thang, Roman. Jewel was annoyed with me because every time she tried to talk to me, I was somewhere spaced out.

"I'm so sorry girl. I'm just so hype. I really hope things work out between us. He's really everything that I ever asked for," I said.

"Well I'm glad you happy Bitch, but I need my best friend back," Jewel replied.

"I'm sorry- what's up?" I asked.

"So why they saying them cheer bitches got a problem because we want their niggas," she said, "them niggas want us!"

She paused, "These bitches putting shit all on Twitter. Now Daisy all of a sudden became close with them!"

Well, that snapped me back into reality quick. I wouldn't call myself a fighter because I didn't like to fight and when I did, it was rarely because of me- but I will, and I wasn't scared. I most definitely wasn't about to take any type of shit from bitches that hardly knew me.

"So, I just wanna know what Daisy wanna do because she already know it's no problem to get popped on and them bitches see us every day and never do or say shit, so I think it's pressing time," I said.

"You so stupid, but they scary, they always talking shit," Jewel said.

"Well, I'mma need them to keep their thoughts to themselves," I responded.

"Is Ta-Ta here?" my older cousin Marie said.

"Yea, she's in her room asleep- why?" my mom asked.

"I want her to ride with me somewhere real quick," my cousin said.

"Ok, I'll wake her up," my mom said.

On a Saturday morning last summer, my cousin traveled across town to wake me up to address a problem they had with a young girl my age. When I saw Marie, I already knew what the problem was. The day before, we had got into an argument with the same female at our city's "taste of" event. It was the day after the junior prom, and she thought she was the flyest thing walking with her stank-ass outfit and beach curls (not really a style for prom if you ask me). She got the spirit of Twitter fingers over the past couple of days and decided that she wanted to use her 40 characters to write unknown, untrue information because she was never around types of things about my cousins. So, Marie being who she was, asked shorty if there was a problem. Of course, just as females do when they get caught up in their cyberspace thugish ways, she denied that she had any issue. Moments after we left, her Twitter fingers were at it again, and she wrote on her social media "Bitches think they so tuff, but didn't do shit."

Not so lucky for her, Marie got word that she was at a nearby park, so we thought we'd pay her a little visit.

She was in the backseat of my cousins' friend's car. Who was she all bent out of shape over in the first place? Now, Marie was like our older sister and didn't too much play when it came to us, so we were on our way to solve this problem once and for all.

All four of us approached the car asking her what she wanted to do because nobody was gonna go back and forth with her. She looked like she saw a ghost. Then, one of the other females who was around said, "I can't let you guys jump her."

"Oh no, wasn't anybody gonna jump her," Marie said.

"No, Imma just fight her," I said.

She popped up from the back and was like, "I don't even know you, so I'm not about to fight you!"

"Well, you do, however, know my cousins and you felt the need to talk shit about them all over social media. They aren't about to fight no little-ass girl, so that's where I come in," I said.

Everybody was staring in awe at how bold and ready I was.

"There's no need to talk because I don't know you and we're never gonna be friends so get out the car!" I demanded.

Moments went by, and she didn't get out the car. I didn't come out of my sleep for nothing, so I wasn't gonna leave unless I touched somebody. When the door was closed, she talked so much shit about how she was gonna beat my ass, but when the door opened, and I was gonna whoop that ass, she had an excuse -so finally I opened the door myself and smacked her. The girl that was standing over there immediately jumped in between the two of us and shut the door. The girl went fake crazy in the car, and I'm just standing there waiting for her to come out.

"Let her out so I can go home!" I said.

They finally opened the door because she was destroying his car. As soon as the door opened, she stopped going crazy.

"So, what's up?" I said.

"You better be lucky I just got my nails done, or I would beat yo' ass!" she said.

So, I reached down into my pocket and proceeded to hand her some money- "I'll pay for them after I beat yo' ass," I said.

"I don't even know you!" she kept saying.

I learned a long time ago not to force anybody who's scared of you to fight, so we ended up leaving her alone and going home. Of course, she ran back to the internet- and this time we were considered bullies- but she knew not to try it again. She called our male cousin to make sure all beef was off and that she didn't have to watch her back anymore. I didn't like ongoing confrontation and unknown problems, so I was ready to nip this in the bud.

As soon as I saw my, once-upon-a-time associates, I said, "So what's the problem?"

They all looked at me like I was speaking another language.

"Okay so let me help you out," I said, "guess on Twitter me and Jewel are some hoes, and we think we the shit, etcetera etcetera."

"Girl what are you talking about? Don't nobody be thinking about you and Jewel," one of them finally said.

I didn't have a Twitter account, so I really didn't know whether or not the tweet was written, but I trusted Jewel enough to know she wouldn't tell me no bullshit.

"Well that's the talk, and I'm just confused because I don't remember any of you being around in my personal life and as far as me thinking I'm 'the shit,'- I thought that was pretty apparent," I said.

My mouth was so slick that if they did have any ounce of "like" for me, my mouth took care of that.

"Well you will know if we had a problem or not- you will hear it straight from us," she said.

"Ok great," I said in my best Becky voice. I often approach situations alone because I'm not with that 'she had to put on a show/ she only tuff with her friends' shit.

Thinking that was the end of drama for the day, I walked into my house after school and prepared to have a relaxing rest of the day because I didn't have to work. The mood was pretty tense in the house between my mom and my sister's dad, so I already knew an argument was brewing. Surprisingly, the day was quiet enough for me to take a nap and later on that night we all watched a movie in the living room. Shortly after, my step-dad entered the room and started something out of the clear blue with my mom. She ignored him and just let him talk. I could tell she was tired of always arguing with him. He left and went into the kitchen for a long while.

"I'm sorry that you guys have to deal with this; please learn from this and never deal with a man like that ever," my mom said.

Me and my sisters just sat there without a response. We had our own opinions, but we knew better to just sit there and let her talk. He overheard her telling us that, and he came in with a wet rag and hit my mother in the face. That triggered me- I hated sitting there listening to them argue and being told to "stay in a child's place" when I wanted to get involved, but this time I didn't care. I was not gonna' sit around and let anybody put their hands on my mother no matter who it was or how I felt about her decisions.

I jumped up, and so did my sisters. My mom immediately told us to sit down. She jumped up and pushed him down to the ground, followed up by a couple blows to the face. She was screaming for us to pack all of our stuff so we could leave. Shook by what I thought of was good news, my sisters and I ran to our rooms and packed as much clothes as we possibly could and loaded them all into the car. We didn't have a place in mind to go but, my mom knew she was never going back there. The whole time we were loading up, my sisters' dad talked the most shit he ever talked.

All I did was laugh at his sad ass, and he walked up to me and said, "You're happier than a gay guy with a bag of dicks."

"Truuuue," I responded.

That just made him angrier. I was a very emotional person, and although I laughed everything off, it hurt down to my soul to live with someone who spoke to us like we were someone off the street. That day, we moved in with my cousin Rose and her mom until we found somewhere to live.

A month and a half later, we moved into my great grandfather's old home on my father's side. He passed away a few years prior and left the house to my grandfather, so he didn't charge my mom a lot to move in. She could save to move somewhere more to her liking. My mom was secretly going over to our old house spending weekends there with my sisters' dad, which annoyed everyone involved in the situation. I hated the fact that she was falling back in but I thought maybe things would be a little better now that we had our own house. We wouldn't have to witness anymore arguing or fighting.

But, that too was short lived. He started off by staying the night here and there. He couldn't afford the place we were at, so he moved in. I was pissed. One, because me and Rome grew closer since our date and I was getting use to him coming over and staying as long as he wanted, and two, because there was so much peace and family time in the house. I think my mom felt sorry for him the day he moved in because he threw himself down the stairs as a threat if she didn't let him move in with us.

My life was all around consistent with friends, family, and my new boo. There was occasionally back and forth between my crew and the cheer bitches, but that wasn't about anything at all. I was open to Roman about my home situation. He knew how much I didn't want to be there, so we started going to his house after work. Things with him and me were going pretty well except the fact that we hadn't made it official. I didn't really press the issue because we were doing everything an "official couple" would do- and he also became my first lover. It wasn't until Talia put me on to the fact that his ex-girlfriend found out that he was dealing with me and wanted him to give second thoughts about them. This, of course, made me furious; I put in work to be more than just his friend, and our chemistry was good. She would come to our job whenever she was in town, and I'd always "help" her out with her order. There were a couple of times she stayed until he was on break so she could have a "conversation" with him. If it wasn't for Talia, their conversations would've been rudely interrupted with my fist.

Bella was always in class when I needed her, and she was the only one who I would allow to give me advice on things in my life. I sent her an "SOS" text. When I spoke to her, she told me to talk to him about his relationship with his ex and to not react to anything too quickly before I knew the situation. Bella said that she was moving back to town since she finally was able to transfer here to our city's university. I was relieved. She, too, was going through a bit of turmoil between her and her new lover so at this point, her moving back was good for the both of us.

We proceeded normally. Our text message feed usually went something like this:

Wyd

I'm on my way

I'm ready

I'm here

It became a routine. I would spend most nights at Rome's place. If I was tired of him, or vice versa, or if we wanted to spend time with our friends or had a family event, we didn't see each other.

I was nervous. I didn't know how to approach the situation in a calm way. I was scared that what I had to say might ruin chances of us actually being a couple. He lived with his parents and two brothers. They were pretty nice, so I kind of added them to the conversation to ease some tension. Their house was designed like a two-family house, except upstairs had everything but a kitchen. It was like their own personal man cave.

We all sat in the living room and laughed and joked around like we normally would. His younger brother, who was my age, was dating somebody new and he asked me if I knew her and wanted me to tell him everything about her. I used that to break the ice because I did, in fact, know the female- and let's just say she knew a lot of people as well.

"Would you let her still be friends with her ex?" I asked.

Roman looked dead at me. He knew I was talking about him. His brothers knew too.

"No, because if that's the case they should try and work it out," his younger brother replied.

The eldest brother cut right to the chase and asked me why I asked the question. I was honest. Roman just started at me.

"Well in their case," he said, trying to defend his brother- "they've been together for a really long time, and they were friends first, so they are always gonna be friends even if they aren't messing around anymore."

"Well I agree with baby bro," I said, "I think that if they're cool enough to still be friends, then old feelings might resurface- I just don't trust it."

At first, I was happy that Roman sat there and said nothing. But, as we got deeper into the conversation, I felt like he should have chimed in at some point to at least defend the side that applied to him. But, because of his silence, I didn't get any answers. That made me so mad that I didn't even stay that night. The only thing now was to go off his actions.

It didn't take that long for Bella to finally come back. I forgot to tell her that we didn't live in the same place the day she wanted to come over. She was sad that I didn't live so close anymore, so we took advantage of that. We spent the whole day together, and before we knew it, it was dark. That night it was really warm out, so we decided to take a walk. That side of town, though not very safe, was the best side of town to walk around on because everything was open and you'd at least run into one person you knew. That night our friendship escalated to a new level. We talked about everything under the sun- from family situations to our love life. We discovered that we handled a lot of situations very similar. She also noticed and called me out on how I was dealing with the Roman situation.

"You've changed," she said, "it's not bad, but I know you're putting up with certain things because of how you and Dame ended."

"Yea," I agreed, "but I sort of lost sense of what I should allow or what I should put up with. It was sort of easier with Dame because he was always around- if we weren't at school he would be at my house, so I never felt like I had to worry about what he was doing- and look how that turned out."

I always followed the saying, 'If you want different results, you have to do something different. I don't think he would be so open with me about his ex if he was gonna go back to her or didn't want to hurt me."

"But that still don't make it right Star; you shouldn't be in a situation where you have to feel like that," she said.

"I guess I'm not trying to face the reality that this female is a problem," I said.

With the discomfort at home, I at least wanted my love life to be straight- that was my escape.

121

"Yea, but you have to especially because that was your first," she said.

I was taken aback because I had never gotten around to telling her or Jewel.

"How'd the hell you find out," I said, "I mean not that I wasn't gonna tell you or anything, but how'd you guess?"

"Girl, it's so obvious," she said laughing, "you wouldn't be worrying about his whereabouts- or this chick for that matter- if y'all situation hadn't escalated to that level."

"The Ta I know would've dropped him like a bad habit as soon as you heard about another chick" she continued.

"I'm just trying to not make that same mistake again. I'm tired of my feelings being hurt," I said.

"That's why it's important for you guys to have this talk because as a female you can't help but to catch feelings after having sex. Chemically, we release the same hormone when we give birth as when we have sex. We start getting attached," she said.

Sometimes, I wondered how she knew the shit she knew. She was right though; I was catching feelings and scared to lose him. I never thought that sex would have a big part in that. I didn't want to spend too much time in my feelings, so I switched the convo to her. Honestly that night I don't remember anything she was doing; I kept replaying in my head how I was gonna handle my situation.

The next day, I asked Talia about what I should do with the Roman situation. She said the same thing as Bella.

"Especially because she keeps showing up here, it's just not worth the fight," she advised.

You're right," I said.

Talia's boyfriend overheard us talking and chimed in. "I can put you on with my boy if you want," he said.

I smiled' "no thanks- I'm fine.

"I know you ain't talking about Robert," Talia said.

"Chill, you and Robert need to cut that shit out and get along," he replied.

I told him I was fine, and I laughed it off. Talia and her boyfriend always got into it over the simplest things.

"ANYWAYS," Talia said, "I like Roman and everything, but you're my friend and no matter how nice of a guy Roman is he can't get away with stuff like that."

She was right, so during the duration of the rest of my workday, I allowed myself to take a step back and think. I was stuck in between what I felt and how I should be treated. I was afraid of acting like a little girl, and I considered the fact that he told me about his ex, instead of hiding it. I texted him that I wanted to talk to him later on that night. He agreed without hesitation- unlike most men.

I daydreamed the rest of the time at work. The regular customers noticed that I was a bit spaced out.

"Are ya tired?" the old man who orders a small strawberry banana smoothie with a protein shot every day said.

"Yea, I had a long day," I said.

"I saw that you guys were busy and you still managed to hold it together," he replied.

"That's what we do best," Talia said.

He didn't realize how much that innocent conversation influenced my next move. I got to thinking. Out of all the things I endured, I always managed to keep it together. I realized that's what I'd always done. The worst thing known to mankind, in my opinion, is feeling like crap inside. To "keep it together," I've learned to subconsciously suppress any yucky feeling that I had and avoid talking about it. I needed some relief.

When I got home, I did the regular routine when I was getting ready to see him. When I was in middle school, I was really close with my health teacher, Ms. Brown. I remember I had a crush on a boy and he didn't like me back. She noticed how sad I was and she told me the best revenge is looking good. I took pride in that ever since. I made sure for this occasion I looked like the sexiest girl who was ever about to go to sleep.

About nine that night, I got a text from Roman saying that he was outside. Since this was about me ending it with him, I wanted us to talk outside in the car. When I got in the car, it was a long awkward silence. He broke that silence by asking how work was. I told him it was super busy and he was happy he wasn't there.

I took a deep breath and jumped right in, "I'm really starting to like you, and I especially love that you're mindful of my home situation and you let me stay at your house all the time."

He cut me off. "You're there because I want you to be- not because of anything else."

I smirked because I didn't know whether to take that as compliment or an insult. So, I disregarded it.

"Well it's appreciated," I said, "however, I don't like the fact that you're still friends with your ex."

"That's problematic for me because you guys were in a relationship for a long time and I can't compete with that so I think we should just stop seeing each other," I continued.

Bracing myself for what he was going to say, I took another deep breath.

"Do you know why we broke up?" he asked.

"No," I said, even though Talia had filled me in.

"This would actually be the second time we broke up," he said, "when she went to college she called me and told me she was in love with someone else. When that failed, I gave her a second chance. The next semester, she turned around and did the same thing. I'm never going back to her. We can only be friends."

"The fact that you still let her be a part of your life after all of that lets me know that you still care-I don't know, I just don't trust that. I dealt with a situation like this, and I know from experience that you should close one door before you open the next. So, to protect myself I think we should just be cool," I said.

Without warning, I got out the car and went back into the house. I didn't want to do it, but I knew that I didn't want to deal with that again. I felt weird inside like I was making a mistake, but I knew my friends would help me tuff it out.

I sluggishly walked to the bathroom, took my clothes off and turned the shower on until the water got steamy. I sat on the toilet until I found the perfect song to sit in my sorrow in. Prayed for strength and discipline, then got into the shower singing Cupid by Sam Cooke. I never understood why the human race does things to make situations worse because this song only made me cry.

My attitude was so fucked up at this point in my life that I didn't care who ain't like me. Bella put me D to a picture of Roman and his ex on social media wearing matching boots on Thanksgiving Day. I was pissed, but I didn't press him because that's what I told him to do. I just hate that men have to lie, so they have their cake.

That picture is partly responsible for the way I was acting. I was very short with people and put on a full armor of 'I don't give a fuck.' The drama at school escalated. It started to become my crew vs. everybody else. Oddly, I think people didn't like us because of how much we had each other's backs, and no one could come between it. We were also extra over the top. We walked the halls with our heads held high like we owned the joint and we always were clowning around. That attitude lasted the rest of the school year and into that summer.

It was really awkward at work, being that Roman was there. When we worked shifts together, we tried as hard as we possibly could to not speak to each other. It broke my heart, and I kept all that emotion inside. Being that he was my first and he knew it, I expected more from him. At least a word or two regardless of what was going on between us, but no, not one word, just eight hours of us avoiding each other and dead silence. I kept a mean poker face- then went home and cried, prayed, meditated and repeated day in and day out. I never vented to anyone, having learned by now that my friends were shallow. Jewel, in a general sense, just told me to bust a dutch and forget his ass. Bella probably would've given me some good advice, but she was worried about image and how crazy I'd look if I showed emotion in front of him, and then think up a mind game to play. Somehow, all of our conversations would end up about something about her. Usually, I'd want that from both of them. I liked how they got over things and how simple it was for Jewel to say, "Fuck it," and how complex Bella made me realize everything was.

Truthfully, I wanted and needed to figure things out on my own. I needed undivided attention and depth with a little bit of 'fuck it' at the end. I didn't find that in either of my best friends, so I often dealt with things alone. That was my way of being stoical in my friendships. Although my friendships didn't fulfill my emotional needs, I accepted and valued them for what they were- going home and doing my own thing worked better for me.

I missed Roman the most at night when it was time for bed. I was still annoyed with the fact that my sisters' father found his way back into our space. Yes, I isolated myself in my room every time an argument would brew, but I would still be on edge the whole time listening for any sign of physicality in case I had to come out and jump in. At this point, Mia learned to sleep through the arguments because she knew my mom would forgive him the next day. Sady would still cry or try to break it up herself. If it got too bad, she would find her way to my room, and we would pray together. The relationship between me and my mom got worse because I kept losing respect for her. Any conversation we had would result in an argument. She gave me unwanted advice about men and how I can't keep one. I was starting to think that she was taking all her frustrations out on me because it was easier. She clearly didn't know how to handle her own bad situation and because she's my mother anything that I said in my defense was considered disrespectful.

With drama in every part of my life, I was starting to fall into a deep depression because I couldn't find an escape anywhere. I couldn't even muster up the energy to keep a steady prayer life. I put the 'B' in bitch. Holding everything in made me extremely bitchy and less receptive to things that didn't go my way. I was beginning to understand what it meant that the only person that can make you happy is yourself. I just didn't know where to start.

"Hold thou the good; define it well; for fear divine philosophy should push her beyond her mark and be procuress to the lords of hell," - Alfred Tennyson.

CHAPTER THREE

Fear

Fear /FIR/
An unpleasant emotion caused by the belief that
someone or something is dangerous, likely to cause pain
or a threat.

"Fear is pain arising from the anticipation of evil," - Aristotle.

I was scared. Aheem threw himself down the stairs in the middle of the night.

"Please," he cried, "don't kick me out!"

"You're crazy!" my mom yelled back.

"I just want to be with my family!" he said.

I could've thrown up right there on the spot at the sound of those words. I couldn't recall a time we ever felt like a family with him.

131

The stairs were located right outside my door. It sounded like a tree hit our house when he hit the bottom of our stairs. I ran out of my room quickly because I thought their fight turned physical.

"What's going on?" I yelled.

"Nothing- this motherfucker out here acting crazy," she replied casually.

"You should've never let him back in," I said.

"Shut the fuck up and stay in a child's place. That's your problem now," she scolded.

All I heard after that was blah blah blah as I backed into my room, heart heavier than it was previously. Somehow, her anger toward him transferred to anger toward me. The focus on whatever her and Aheem were arguing about before grew smaller and smaller the more she yelled at me for my comment. I just sat on my bed and cried with disappointment.

"Here she goes again, taking frustrations out on me," I thought.

After a while, I stopped crying and just stared into space for about an hour-- daydreaming, slowly removing my thoughts out of reality. As my depression increased, all I wanted to do at the end of every day was go home, get into my bed and daydream. I could control everything that was happening in the world inside my head. It was my secret escape from reality. When I couldn't think of anything else to daydream about, I would reach out to my friends for a different kind of pick-me-up. I knew talking or being around my friends would take my mind off my own feelings.

Sometimes, me and Bella would go on escapades, do drive-bys, and pull up on her lover. Sometimes, we would have long conversations about our relationship with God; we even went to church together. Occasionally we would slide through a bar and get a drink.

With things being pretty stagnant at school with all of the drama, me and Jewel finally had time to have a conversation without mentioning anything that transpired between the two groups. One of the things I loved most about Jewel was that we could have a 4 to 5-hour conversation without mentioning the same thing twice. We talked about things from comedy to fashion. We had lots of inside jokes from using the growing social media comic's lingo when referring to certain things and situations. I remember when we tried to figure out what we were going to wear to the end of the school year party.

"Let's see- how I'ma kill 'em," Jewel said in her best Benji Brown's "ki ki" voice.

"Girl I haven't even thought about what I was gonna wear," I replied.

"There's never anything at the mall," she said.

"Girl I'm just gonna take my ass right to Forever 21 and see what they have there," I said.

The last day of junior year finally arrived, and it fell on a Friday. Party time. Me and Jewel linked with another member of our squad, Tasia, and two of Jewel's other friends that we really didn't hang out with in school.

This guy who didn't have an ID to get into a club himself started to throw parties at his house every weekend. He'd been promoting the 'end of the school year' party for some time now, and this would be the first party we attended without the older girls we hung out with. They always looked out for us when we went to parties, so we got drunk freely. Me and Jewel ended up wearing bodysuits and heels, looking like some young Thundercats. I ran into Talia's boyfriend Raheem at the party; he was alone as far as I could tell, but I had to hold my girl down and ask some questions- you know, make sure he wasn't out there disrespecting her.

"Where's Talia?" I asked.

"She's at home with an attitude probably; I'm here getting some peace," he said.

I chuckled. "Don't say that; whatever's going on I'm sure y'all will work it out, you always do.

"Man, I'm not worried about that- she'll get over it," he said, "so who you here with? What's up with you and ol' boy?"

"I'm here with some friends from school, and I don't know what's up with ol' boy- but I'm chilling," I replied.

"Well Star, like I told you, I can put you on with my boy whenever you ready," he offered.

I laughed. "I'll keep that in mind."

We got so wasted that night; by the time the party ended, we were all slumped on the couch. Our male friend Boss had dropped us off as he always did with any other party, and just like any other party, if we weren't ready by 2 am, it was over for a ride home. Boss was a genuine friend though. The guys at our school were jealous of Boss because he was always around the ladies- not just our crew, but just about every female in the school. He was the only guy in school who had a car ever since he started high school, so he always had that advantage over the other guys. Boss was a really cool dude to hang out with. He was a pothead like the rest of us, so we always smoked together while riding around the town. Occasionally, when he was feeling generous, he would take us out to eat. What was even better was that he didn't try to come on to us. You couldn't convince any of the other fellas that that wasn't the case though. Boss benefited us in a deeper way than we realized. He showed us that not every guy you meet is trying to get in your pants.

We woke up- and it was way past 2 am. We tried to call Boss and just like we expected, he didn't answer. I tried to call one of my cousins to see if they were around, but none of them answered either. The only other person at the party was Raheem. He was waiting for his ride. "What the hell y'all still doing here?" he said.

"We fell asleep, now we can't find a ride home," we said.

"Well shit, my boy Rob about to pull up- I'll see if he can give y'all a ride," he said.

Jewel, Tasia and I were cool with that idea, as long as we weren't gonna be stuck at some random guy's house. Jewel's other friends didn't feel comfortable getting a ride with someone they didn't know. That was understandable, so we didn't put up a fight. We just left. Come to find out, one of her friends was fucking with the promoter, so she had other plans anyway.

Raheem's friend pulled up in a nice, all-white Impala, and he didn't look half bad himself. "This my boy Rob," Raheem said as we all piled up in his backseat. Rob turned around and said hi to the three of us when we finally got settled. We bashfully said hi back. None of us had got perms, so we looked like a hot sweaty mess. We weren't that far from my house, so I expected to be home quick.

"I gotta stop somewhere real quick," Rob said.

Me and my friends all gave each other that look like, "What you mean?" He interrupted our thoughts by asking us if we smoked or not.

"Yea they smoke," Raheem said.

I texted Raheem because I didn't want Rob to hear. *Where the hell we going?*

He responded quickly. *Chill Ta! Y'all good. Y'all with me. Just relax.*

I reassured my friends that everything was ok. As the blunt was being rotated, Rob blasted *Take Me Away*, by Kyana. He had it on repeat while we drove to the outskirts of the city.

Now, my first thought was that Rob was some type of drug dealer and he had to hurry up and catch a lick or something. Then I thought these niggas were trying to be slick and take us to a hotel or something. Both thoughts were wrong. We pulled up to this complex of beautiful homes deep in the suburbs and into the driveway of one of the most beautiful homes I'd seen- outside of my grandfather's house.

"Okay y'all can get out," Rob said.

Jewel quickly chimed in, "Ummm, where the fuck we at?"

The guys were surprised because she hadn't made a sound since she got in the car.

"This my boy crib," Raheem said.

"Ok and what are we doing at ya boy crib, its three something in the morning," she asked.

"My aunt won't mind if y'all stay here. I'll just bring you guys home in the morning," Rob said.

Then suddenly, it clicked. This was Rob, as in Robert, the same nigga Raheem was trying to set me up with ever since he heard about me and Roman.

"Raheem, what the hell are we doing here, you ain't say nothing about this. It's mad late, and we're all sweaty and shit!" I yelled.

"Y'all can take a shower here and shit," Raheem said.

I was so upset because he acted like he didn't see the problem. We pouted for about five minutes before we decided to get out the car. We made a quick pact that we were gonna stay together.

I didn't know what to expect. We walked into a big foyer, and everything was decorated so nicely. Off to the side, there was a door that led to the basement. Both of the guys led us to that door, and it was like walking down to another living room.

"This is like my little apartment," Rob said.

"We be in this shit lit," Raheem added.

"I see," I replied.

It had two big couches and a TV set up like a mini living room. There was a bar off to the side with every liquor I could think of. In the back, slightly around the corner, were some weights. Me and my girls all sat close by each other on the couch.

"I can bring you guys some towels if you wanna get cleaned up," Rob said, "and I got a new pack of T-shirts if y'all wanna take your stuff off. I don't know what to do about bottoms."

"This nigga think he slick," I thought.

"I don't mind that," Tasia said surprisingly.

"Bitch, we ain't free balling," I whispered.

"Listen, Ta. I'm tired as fuck. I will turn my shits inside out. I don't give a fuck. Shit, we can turn our jumpsuits inside out and wear them as bottoms," she said.

"Ok, I guess. I just wanna go to sleep," I said.

"Ok, can you show us to the bathroom?" I said to Rob.

He handed us three wash clothes and three towels out of his hamper and led us to the top floor where the bathroom was.

"When y'all done, just come straight down. We can roll up, and I'll pour y'all some drinks," Rob said.

"Ok, cool," we said.

We were in the bathroom for about forty-five minutes getting cleaned and talking about what the hell we just got ourselves into. By the time we got all settled, it was getting close to four in the morning. We were up, so we went back downstairs and participated in whatever they had set up for us.

To not make it more awkward than it already was, Raheem sparked up a conversation, and everyone started to loosen up. Rob invited us to go upstairs and smoke outside by the pool. By this time, it was six in the morning but still dark outside. It was late June, so the temperature was still comfortable for a summer night. In the midst of our smoke session, Rob asked me to come upstairs with him to get blankets for everybody. I knew that he just wanted to get some alone time. I followed his lead up the stairs, and when we finally got into a room, he said, "I don't know why you acting like you don't know me."

NOW THAT I HAVE YOUR ATTENTION

"I'm confused," I said.

He just stood there staring at me like he was trying to make me remember. I was too mesmerized by his hazel eyes.

"Summer school," he said interrupting the hypnosis.

I hadn't been to summer school since my freshman year, and that was just so I could be with my friends.

"That way a minute ago. I don't remember everyone in my classes," I said.

"That's crazy because you sat right next to me during math," he said, "and you always wore leggings. I remember because I couldn't stop looking at your ass."

I couldn't stop cheesing; he was so blunt and honest.

"That's crazy- I don't remember you- I'm sorry," I insisted.

"Well I had a brush cut back then, so I probably look a little different," he said.

I sat there and thought about it for a second, and it came back to me. I did remember a fine-ass boy in my math class with pretty eyes and waves. I was so wrapped up in Dame I probably didn't pay too much attention to it.

"I think I do remember you," I said.

He motioned for me to sit on the bed next to him. "I had a crush on you since then," he said.

I looked at him and smirked. "You lying."

"No! Dead-ass," he said, "I walked by the smoothie joint and noticed you, I've been trying to get 'Heem to put me on, cuz I knew his shorty worked there."

"Oh okay, that's what's up," I said shyly.

He moved a little closer. "So why don't you have a man?"

"I don't know- I just haven't found that right one yet," I said.

"Looks like we in the same boat," he said.

I chuckled shyly.

"You don't have to sleep downstairs next to everybody," he offered, "you can sleep up here."

I just sat there quiet, I wanted to be in a bed after being up all night, but I didn't want Jewel and Tasia to feel uncomfortable.

"Ok, let me just make sure my friends are okay," I said.

"Ok, cool," he said.

We walked downstairs to the back deck where we left them, and there was no one there. We walked downstairs to the basement and discovered Jewel and Tasia on the big couch knocked out, and Raheem on the smaller couch knocked out. I put the blankets we brought back down over Jewel and

Tasia, and we just left Raheem on the couch how he was. We walked back upstairs to the bed. I was so nervous. I didn't know what to expect. I got right into the bed and under the covers. I closed my eyes with hopes that he wouldn't try anything. I don't remember when I fell asleep, but I remember when I woke up.

My eyes popped right open. The weight of Rob's body on my abs startled me.

"What the hell is he trying to do," I thought.

He slowly started moving further and further down my abs to the top of my hot pocket. I clinched up. I felt the anxiety coming on. "What are you doing?" I asked.

"I bet you've never been ate like this in your life," he said.

"Ate? What the hell does that mean," I wondered.

Before I could go into a panic, his tongue began moving back and forth across my clit. I was instantly paralyzed. I sat there, legs spread and mouth open in complete shock at how satisfying this was. In twenty minutes, I learned that a female could come from oral sex. I knew in my head that the other thing was coming next, and I wasn't mentally prepared for that.

∞

Uncle Norm led me downstairs to the back room in my grandma's house, where nobody went. "Ok, now I'll be right outside the door. Just let me know you're done," he said.

"Ok," I said quietly. As I began to take my clothes off, I kept my eyes on the door just in case anybody tried to come in. As I scanned the door, I noticed his feet at the bottom. He was blocking the door, and that somehow made me feel safe. I turned around toward the mirror continuing to take my clothes off. I took some time to examine my body.

"I look nothing like those women in them magazines," I thought.

Why did he want me to do it? I started to get scared again. I wanted to leave. I knew something wasn't right; the way he spoke about my body didn't match with what I was looking at. I had to find a way to get out of there without making him mad. I put my clothes back on and knocked on the door from the inside. He walked into the room all sneaky-like.

"So, are you ready now?" he asked.

"I'm almost ready. I just think I need another day of practice. I want it to be just like the magazine," I said.

I heard my cousin Holdin coming up the stairs calling my name.

"You better not say anything," Uncle Norm whispered.

"TA TA, Grandpa gave us some money to go to the store-you better hurry up!" Holdin yelled.

His search for me was short- lived and Uncle Norm began whispering to me aggressively that I better have all my shit together by tomorrow. When he let me out the room, I ran downstairs as fast as I could and bumped into Holdin.

"What's wrong with you?" he said. I wanted to just burst out in tears and tell him everything that was going on. I didn't want things to get worse, so I didn't tell him. Besides, what power did Holdin have that would make this go away?

"I was in the bathroom, and I heard you say we were going to the store and I don't wanna get left."

❦

Before Rob could get close enough to slide up in me, I quickly rolled over and started hyperventilating. Fear began to creep up on me as I thought of the consequences of my panic. I got scared. I was scared that he would be angry at me because I didn't want to give him anything in return. I was scared because I wasn't ready for that next step, and didn't think I would ever be. I was also scared that I would be the laughing stock between him, Raheem and all of their friends. I was even more scared of what my friends would think if I decided to have sex with him.

"What's good with you?" he said.

"I just don't know if I should do this," I said between breaths, "we just met."

"Well, you wasn't just saying that a few minutes ago," he said in an irritated tone.

That's when I snapped and yelled back, "I also didn't ask for any of that a few minutes ago either!"

I decided right there and then that this wasn't gonna be one of those times I had to explain to a man the reason why sex was hard for me.

"Look I'm not trying to front on you or anything, but you're not about to act like I used you for some head. You made your way down there on your own, and now you putting an expectation on me like I owe you something. You never once asked me if I've done this before, so you obviously think I'm some type of easy target," I said.

We sat there quiet on the bed for a few minutes then he said, "C'mere."

I didn't move.

"I get it," he said. "I wasn't thinking anything fucked up, I just saw something I liked, and I went for it."

"Interesting," I replied.

"No, for real," he said, "I like your vibe and everything. You seem like a good girl, and if we can't be anything else, I still wanna be your friend."

I rolled my eyes and turned over. He left the room, and I fell asleep.

The next morning, we woke up to the smell of breakfast. His aunt figured out he had company and instead of cursing us all out for being in her house, she had our plates already made by the time we got ourselves together. To our surprise, she asked if we had a good time and that next time we could get in the pool if we wanted. We just thought she was being nice until it became our weekend routine throughout the entire summer. It would literally be times when Jewel, Tasia and I would be at a party, get bored mid-turn up, and wanted to go to Rob's house. For me, it was a sweet escape. I grew sweet on Rob over time. His presence was especially clutch. What I liked about him the most was that it didn't matter how late at night it was or where we I was, he'd come and get me. If I wanted Jewel and Tasia there- which was 90% of the time- he would go get them too, no matter how late or where they were.

Ever since our first encounter, he always made sure I was comfortable. If that meant treating my friends as well as he treated me, then so be it. Of course, because of that, he gained their hearts as well.

"I like Rob," Tasia would always say out of the blue.

"Me too," Jewel always added.

"Yea he's a cool dude," I would reply.

That was always how the conversation started when they were trying to convince me to take him more seriously.

"I don't know if I want to be serious with anyone right now," I said, "I like how things are going."

"I know damn well you not still worried about Roman's ass," Jewel said.

Ugh. I hated that she could see right through me. "No. I'm not worried about him, but I'm not about to just jump into anything with anyone," I lied.

Things at work were still awkward. Talia didn't approve of how much time I was spending with Rob, and I was nervous to talk to her about it. They hated each other.

We finally had a moment alone at work to talk freely without Roman around.

"I can't stand him, TA," she said.

"But why though- he's actually a really cool dude," I said.

"He always tries to get Raheem to leave me," she continued.

"But why though," I asked, "what transpired that he has to say something like that?" I asked.

She gave me a stank look.

"I'm not trying to take his side or anything," I said, "but when I bring you up to him, he gives me the same general shit that you do. I would actually like for all of us to hang out together one day."

"Why? He's not your boyfriend," she replied.

I rolled my eyes- "Ugh, forget it" I said.

I later found out that the beef between them was because Talia and Raheem went through a period where they were in some serious turmoil and Raheem would talk so badly about her to Rob that it made him not like her. But, the gag is Raheem and Talia never broke up. This is why you don't talk badly about the person you're dealing with until you know for sure that you won't be dealing with them again. Whoever you vent to will always feel some type of way about that person after you forgive. Talia soon after got her revenge. She put his then-girlfriend on to some foul shit that he was doing. After that, it went downhill from there.

"I use to be cool with her though," Rob would say, "but she always doing some lame shit."

I heard that Roman was leaving our job because he found a better one. I still had some type of hope that he and I would reconnect. Rob and I wasn't a couple so he wouldn't have been an issue if Roman had a change of heart. Rob was a space filler in all actuality. His vibe was cool, and he treated me and my friends like princesses, but Roman fit the description of everything I'd ever wanted. I didn't want to leave that situation without knowing 'what if.'

One day at work, I asked him if we could have a conversation sometime soon. He agreed, and when I went home that night, I wrote down everything I wanted to say to him.

"What's the worst that can happen- if I am actually honest," I wondered, "he's leaving the job anyway."

I did everything I could that summer to not be home. I either stayed the night at someone's house, or I stayed out so late that all I did was come home and sleep. I lost a tremendous amount of respect for my mom after she let Aheem back in the house. I wasn't trying to be in a position where I had to have any dialogue with him. I feared that if I came in contact with him, I would lash out on him because that's how much I hated him being there. It took the Father, Son and Holy Ghost for me not to budge when they started arguing. I didn't even want to give her the satisfaction of knowing that I cared.

Jewel and Tasia made sure I barely was home that summer. We were either with Rob and Raheem, or we were smoking with Boss and his friends. Other than that, I was at work. I would occasionally link with Bella, but Jewel got jealous every time I canceled a plan with her to link with Bella. Bella wasn't too much tripping off of us spending time together; she had reconnected with another one of her younger friends that summer and they were working on rebuilding their friendship. I didn't mind either. I knew with Bella she would've made me face the hurt and frustration I was feeling at some point, but with Jewel and Tasia all they wanted to do was have fun and party.

That may not have been what I needed, but it was what I wanted. I didn't want to think about my fears. I didn't want to be around anyone who was gonna make me deal with what I was feeling. That still wasn't enough. As soon as I found out Roman was leaving, on came that anticipated fear of losing him forever. I didn't want to sound desperate, but I wanted him to know that I always expected us to come back to each other. I wanted to start my senior year off knowing exactly who my friends were and rock out with the same guy. I was still hoping for that 'high school sweetheart' fairytale.

The beginning of my senior year gave me the same chills as when I started my freshman year. I was hoping any beef I had was over with because they wasted no time telling us that if we got into a fight, it was over for senior prom and graduation. I was pleased to hear that Daisy went to another school, my old high school. It would've hurt me to fight someone I once cared about, and by this time the amount of shit she was talking was liable to get her popped on site. All I can think of was how much shit she was gonna talk about me to the people we both knew. I didn't care though; she was the shiesty one in this situation. I wasn't too much worried about the other bitches though; they dragged their issues with us from junior year to senior year but didn't do a damn thang. Day in and day out, my crew stayed unbothered.

Senior year was already painted out to be a breeze as far as actual school work went. We barely had any classes, so about halfway through the day me and Jewel walked to her house and just chilled. Sometimes, her mother would leave us my favorite meal to heat up. I loved her baked chicken, rice, and gravy. The chicken literally fell-off-the-bone. We binge- watched Pretty Little Liars and Switched at Birth damn near every day.

Not to my surprise though, it wasn't long before the beef got bigger and bigger, like a snowball rolling down the side of a snow-covered hill. Of course, it grew on social media, and Daisy had her parts in it. It was one of the things where a group of people came together solely because they didn't like the same person. The message relayers were the same guys they were mad about in the first place. It blew my mind that Daisy had so much energy when she knew there was a slim chance of her seeing us. By the way, they talked about how 'better than everyone else' we thought we were. It became clearer and clearer that jealousy was the battery in their backs.

A girl I grew up with. Renee, who went to my cousin's day-care- came to my high school in the middle of senior year. She ended up being friends with the same girls who had a problem with us. Being who she was, she got involved and tried to play peacemaker, but of course, that was an epic fail. It wasn't long before her name started circulating and now she was the blame for the beef. She also had most of her classes with them, so every day went like this: I would be sitting in the library with either Tasia or our other friend Liberty waiting for Jewel to get done with her last class so we could leave. I would receive a text from Renee saying that the girls was talking some type of shit, so right before the bell would ring, me and my crew would be waiting outside their classroom door. Most of the time, they walked out of the room, shocked that we were right there, saying nothing, continuing to their regularly scheduled programming. Other times, there was dialogue.

Then I got tired. As soon as I saw one, I attacked. It got broken up quickly by mutual parties, but the commotion carried on to the bottom floor. Jewel, Tasia, Liberty and I got pulled into one administrator's office, and the other girls got pulled into another. They gave us the final reminder to cut the bullshit or everything that made senior year special was going to be taken away from us. We agreed, barely making it to the Hundred Days Dance.

The next senior event was the senior dinner. It hadn't really been any static the months leading up to it, and me and Rob was still spending time together heavily. Roman never left our old job, so the pressure for us to have that final talk was gone. We had gotten to a point where we could have normal conversations again, and he wasn't too much feeling the fact that another guy had my attention.

We had our senior dinner at the Doubletree Hotel. The ballroom was set up so nicely, with the dance floor in the middle separating two sections. Of course, we sat on opposite sides of the ballroom from the people we didn't mess with. Dinner went well, everyone looked nice, and we started flicking it up. It wasn't until it was time to hit the dance floor when I realized how music correlates with emotion. *Did It on 'Em*, by Nicki Minaj, came on, and it started some shit. You would've thought we had drunk a whole bottle of something by the way we bum-rushed the dance floor to scream at the top of our lungs the lyrics to that song.

The dance floor was but so big. Somebody from our crew bumped into somebody from the other crew. We immediately got in each other's faces, screaming the lyrics at each other, trying to refrain from hitting each other. Liberty's boyfriend, who was another one of our male friends, jumped in the middle of everybody who seemed to be getting a little too close. By the time the song was over, there was only one person in their crew still on the dance floor. She started going off at the mouth. We were so tickled by how mad she was. That did nothing but add fuel to the fire; she cut up so bad that she had to get carried out. At this point, I just wanted to fight and get it over with.

This beef literally lasted for two years without anyone doing anything, and it was becoming exhausting.

When Rob picked me, Jewel, and Tasia up from the dinner, I vented to him about how much I just wanted to end it with a bang. He had a Nas-type of realness to him, so he always had something positive to say or made me look at things from a different perspective, even if it put me in my place. I guess that's why I kept him around. He encouraged us to ignore the message relayers and opened our eyes to the fact that they were as much of a problem as the people telling them things.

"People love stirring the pot just so they can have entertainment," Rob said, "go to school, mind ya business, and don't touch anybody unless somebody touches you. Make sure you guys have each other's backs because after y'all graduate, none of this shit is gonna matter."

Then Jewel went on to state how loyal she was and how I never had to worry about anybody running up on me. I didn't care about that. I knew deep down inside that she wasn't a fighter and I didn't want to bring her to any point I had to prove to myself.

4/20 fell on a Friday that year- getting closer and closer to the end of the school year. We managed to make it to the Senior Superelectives event. We had three more months until graduation. All morning, Liberty was getting text messages from the cousin of the girl who talked the most shit about me. She was trying to set up a date to fight. Now, if I didn't know anything else, I knew never to plan a fight with someone. That wasn't my speed anyway. I had seen too many people go to someone's house to fight and they had a boiling pot of bleach waiting for them at the door. When Lib told me, I was ready to get up right then and there and get it over with. At least twelve different people came up to us about the Twitter rants coming from these girls- and I just had enough.

I got up and walked over to the table where they were sitting and said, "So, what y'all wanna do? When we fighting?"

They tried that whole 'girl what are you talking about thing' but I was over it. I pressed the issue so hard that it resulted in a huge argument in the hallway. Everyone was trying to stop me from attacking and then the century guards came running to break it up. The bitch found that to be the perfect opportunity to try and spit on me. If that ejected saliva would've landed on me, then there would've been a fight right there in the hallway. But, I did make a promise. I swore on my grandmother's grave that there would be an ass whooped that day.

I told Lib to text the same cousin who wanted to plan a fight and tell her that there would be a fight after school. I didn't care what anyone was talking about. She texted Lib back and told her that we was gonna have to wait until the next day because she had to work that day at one. I told her to reply that she was gonna have to pencil me in today because there was no way I was gonna let that disrespect slide.

We heard through the grapevine that they were all leaving school early and making sure their friend was safe. I had other plans. Everyone knew her job was about ten minutes away by foot and a straight shot from our school, so I gathered all my friends and told them if I left immediately, I would be able to catch her before she walked into work whether they decided to roll out or not. At about noon that day, I walked my ass from our high school to her job. My friends were behind me trying to keep up, but I walked ahead of them, mad the whole nine miles. When we reached her and her friends (along with a couple of others) they were surprised that I walked all the way there, so they got off the bus as well.

The girls ran into McDonald's before I could approach anybody. The manager peeped what was going on and kicked them out, so they had no choice but to face the music. I was still a good distance away from them, and I saw they were pulling out their phones to call people. That was the cue for me to get this done and over with.

As my squad was approaching the scene, I ran up to the bitch who had saliva in her throat- and she had fear in her eyes. I began to have a little bit of sympathy for her, so I asked her for the last time.

"So, do you wanna fight or not, cuz I'm done with the bull-shit?"

Completely disregarding what I was talking about, she continued her conversation on her phone saying, "Hold on mom, I'm about to whoop this bi-."

Before she could finish her sentence, I punched her in the face. She threw her phone right in between my eyes, and I fell backward. My squad ran up- and so did hers, but no one jumped in. I don't know why I just thought I was gonna run up and beat her ass real quick, judging from the fear in her eyes, but when my back touched the ground, and she started clawing my face it awoke the beast inside me. All I heard was Siah say, "Get her Star!"

I wrapped my hands around her long weave and used both of our body weight to lift me up. I dragged and punched her repeatedly until her best friend ran up on me on the side. Now, I couldn't tell what was going on around me, but all I knew was I didn't want to get jumped. I wrapped my arms around her weave this time and pulled her while running away from her friend. The cops came, and we separated quickly. Me and my friends ran the other way. Lib got word a little late that we were walking down and she arrived as we were running away. She caught up to us as Siah was telling her the story of what happened; she heard the girlfriend tried to jump in and she went back and fought the girl. The rest of us kept running. Renee and her little sister were also at the scene and recorded the whole thing. I was feeling some kind of way because I fell and no one was on top of the fight to make sure that didn't happen. But the way I lifted my body up after laying flat on the ground like I was the last samurai was pretty cool.

The cops were still on the hunt, and our principal came to the scene. I had to hurry up and get the fuck out of there. The first person I called was Rob; he was on his way. Then I called my mom. She was mad at first because she knew how long lasting this beef was and got mad that I had jeopardized losing prom and not walking the stage. But, when she heard it was spit involved, she knew I did what I had to do. I was suspended of course. When Rob picked me up, he lit a dutch and lectured me the whole way to my aunt's house.

That entire weekend, the video of the fight Lib had was circulating all over social media. She wasn't so lucky with her fight, but it honestly looked like a tie to me. In her defense, she did just walk all the way down there and popped on the first person she saw, which was the girl who tried to jump in my fight. They didn't post my fight because, after Lib's, the administration told people whoever had a video would get suspended as well. So, everything on social media about my fight was "all she did was rag her." I always hated that saying because if that was all I had to do, then it looked like there was a bigger problem than me.

There was a lot of shit talking about how Jewel didn't jump in and how Lib's a real one for going back and fighting the girl who tried it with me. I'm not gonna lie. I played into it for a while, and me and Jewel didn't talk for a few days. But, like I always knew, Jewel wasn't a fighter, and she was my best friend for many other reasons. It honestly didn't faze me. It didn't take long for us to be as thick as thieves again-plus she felt guilty for not doing what Lib did. We came to find out that Lib did that for me- but for other reasons too.

When I came back to school, we had a formal hearing, and as expected, I lost prom and graduation privileges. When they sat us all down, we couldn't even think of a real reason we fought in the first place. Both parties blamed the people who were running back and forth telling us things. The mother of the girl I fought liked how honest I was in the meeting. I explained the buildup and the feeling of just wanting to end it and the point I had to prove to myself- which was I don't take no shit from people. We all left the meeting calm enough to be cordial later on. I had no problem with that. I was stoic enough to be able to fight someone and not hold a grudge afterward. A person might even work their way up to a wave from me in the hallway. So much for that though. Because I was the aggressor, I had to finish my four classes at home for the rest of the school year.

My aunt wasn't really feeling the place she was living in after my grandmother passed away, so she decided to move. She never found a place, so when it came time to move out of the place she was, she had nowhere to go- so they moved in with us. Now, this had me a bit nervous because my family really didn't fuck with Aheem like that- especially since he was the reason we moved in the first place. It wasn't all bad because my scary ass got to sleep with my mom and Aheem got bumped to the couch in the basement.

Not being in school gave me a lot to think about. I reached out to Roman; when we met up, I poured my heart out. I started by letting my guard down and telling him of the dream I always had as a little girl. I told him how I thought we would make a great love song. I was open with how much stress I was under because of prom and graduation. I shared how stupid I felt for fighting someone who I knew deep down inside didn't want a real problem to begin with. I told him how cluttered my house was and how I didn't have time to myself to get my thoughts together. I ended it with an 'as long as we can always be friends, I would be happy.'

He matched my honesty and told me that he didn't expect to like me the way he did knowing he had a situation the whole time. It made him feel guilty that he was my first, and when I broke it off with him, it made it easier for him not to have to face that guilt. He also told me that him and ol' girl decided that it was best they never got back together. That meant we were back in business. We were officially unofficial again. I never really ended anything with Rob. We weren't sexually active. He was more like a best friend. I just stopped answering calls and texts. I would just check in every so often.

Prom season was upon us, and I had gotten over the fact that I couldn't go. Me, Jewel and another one of her friends planned an after party just so I could be a part of something. Jewel's friend had like a million sisters, and one of them told us we could use her spot to have a party. They did a hell of a job promoting it too. Two days before, my mom got a phone call from the principal telling her that they were allowing me to go to prom. So many people were on the list to not graduate on time, so that meant they didn't pay their senior dues. The school had extra plates. I was pissed. I had in my head exactly how I wanted to look and one of the things me and Jewel did when we went to her house after school was look at prom dresses. Two days wasn't enough time to do any of that.

Shopping with Bella for prom had me so excited for my day to come. They told us back in April that I wasn't going to prom, so any money my mom had saved up to get me anything was already spent. Luckily, I had a job, and I knew my dad and grandmother was gonna pitch in. That same day, me and my mom went to a couple of local boutiques to see if I would like anything. Damn near everything we saw looked dirty and ran through. I was about to have a meltdown. We traveled a little outside of our city to see if we had better luck and I managed to find a cute purple little number with a rhinestone corset and a short tulle bottom. My mom bought my shoes and, and my dad sent money for my hair. I wanted a sleek weaved ponytail. That's the only thing that would've matched what I had on. I ended up with a ponytail with a hump in the front. It didn't look bad, but it didn't match what I had on.

I didn't really have time to find a date, and I knew it was over for asking Roman for many reasons. I settled with the one he told me, and that was because of short notice. This white guy in my social studies class that liked me had said he would take me but his grandparents would be upset because I was a black girl. Jewel, Lib, and Tasia had prom dates though; I felt a little left out. As a graduation gift, Jewel's mom paid for a limo and gave us all Applebee's gift cards so we could have dinner before we got there.

Prom was cool--not as exciting as I thought-- but it was a chance for us to dress up and have a good time with our friends. It was the first senior event we went to where there wasn't any beef. Our after-party was every bit of lit. Even the girls we didn't like the entire year, came and had a ball. People on the street saw it and came in along with people from other high schools. I got so drunk that I lost my phone and Jewel was stuck making sure I got home okay. My mom opened the door to Jewel holding up a drunk me crying about how much trouble I was gonna be in because I lost my phone-when the whole time it was in my pocket. That wasn't the first or last time Jewel had to take care of a drunk me.

With my house full and Aheem starting his shit again, I spent most of my nights at Roman's. Aheem made up some shit about Holdin cutting up his sneakers. First off, to the naked eye, they looked normal as fuck. You literally (depending on how far or near sighted you were) had to hold the shoe super close to your face and squint to see what may look like a little piece of an incision. My sisters and I agreed that he was trying to start something with them so my mom would kick them out. He knew he couldn't act like his normal self (getting drunk, breaking shit, starting shit) while they were there, but we all knew it wouldn't be long before his true colors shone bright like a diamond.

Everyone ended up leaving or getting fired from the smoothie joint because we were under new management. I ended up getting a new job at an old people's home working dietary. That job started off cool; I kept quiet most days. The money was an upgrade from the smoothie place. My father came to town the day before I graduated; we didn't get confirmation from any administration until the day of that I could even walk the stage. None of my dad's family showed up from out of town. My grandfather sent money like always, and the rest sent their congratulations via word of mouth.

Me and Jewel had our graduation parties on the same day. Mine was earlier in the day, and hers started right after. It was both a bittersweet occasion because she was moving out of town that summer. Me and Bella would see each other here and there, but I spent most of my time at Roman's house.

Before I knew it, I was starting college. I had changed my mind about being a nurse after learning about all the other stuff I could be when I grew up. The way things were going with me and Roman, my heart's desire was to be the wife of a dentist. That's what he was going to school for. I was so excited about learning though. I always saw myself as the girl who racked up a couple of degrees, drove a nice car and lived in a nice house. Then me, Bella, and Jewel would meet up at a certain time of year on a different island or country. Those were my life goals.

Then I had my first real experience with racism in my social studies class. Go figure. My teacher was a short, stocky, white lady, with long curly hair. She was so proud to have come from Italian roots. The only other Italian, short, stocky lady I knew was my cousin's grandmother on his mom side. My uncle and his mom were together long before we were born, so their side of the family was always like our side. His grandmother played the grandmother role to us also. She wasn't much a cook, but when she made Italian salad with the spinach, provolone cheese, tomato and Italian dressing, it made everybody's stomach happy. She could also bake her ass off. She was so sweet. Other than her biological grand-kids, I was her favorite. She was born in Sicily and moved to our hometown when she was young. They lived in a pre-dominantly black neighborhood, but her mother was racist.

When she got old enough to date and bear children, she married a black man. Her mother got mad and disowned her. Her whole family did. Her children never got to meet their grandmother of the white side of their family. She'd often express how much she hated racism, and she was always one of the first to be outside marching or writing a letter to the highest somebody in a case of injustice. She also told us how divided they were in Sicily.

Sicilians were considered the "niggas" of Italy. Actually, I think the word originated there. That was my first realization on how narcissistic racism is. Anyway, I thought my social studies class was going to be exciting because of how proud my teacher was. Then she opened her mouth and started the class by saying, "Before we get into American History, let me just say before we play the blame game, black people enslaved themselves before white people did."

Everyone in our class, except me, looked at her like they saw Satan himself. I politely rose my hand and said,

Well, let me start off by saying two wrongs don't make a right. Although imitation is the highest form of flattery, it wasn't quite flattering to my ancestors. They actually did a terrible job of imitation. I know you're an American History teacher, so you may not know much about Egyptian civilization, but a big part of its success is because of the ability to adapt to the conditions of the Nile river valley for agriculture. Now if you know anything about agriculture, then you know it's the science of farming, growing crops and the rearing of animals to provide food, wool, and other products. Sounds like a lot of labor, right?

It was dead silent, so I responded to myself:

Right, I would imagine you'd need people--shit, damn near everybody-- to have a part in order to have a series of successful civilizations like the Egyptians. Now, we can go back and forth all day on whether or not they were 'beating' them to do a job that would now be illegal under child labor laws, but what I do know is that after they were done with that hard labor, they went back home to their families. There weren't any plantations and personal maids. There were no lynchings, depriving people of food, water, clothes, education and language, and no ripping families apart so they wouldn't know where they came from. So, if YOU wanna play the blame game Mrs., I do blame the makings of America for oppression.

"Is that all Ms. Robinson?" she said.

"Actually, yes," I replied, and then proceeded to get up and walk out of her class, never to return again. I always wondered why some people who weren't affected by slavery felt personally attacked when it came to the subject. It's not like they were the slave master and thought up the idea to oppress a whole race of people. But, it is comments like those that make people outside the white race feel like victims because racism and oppression are still very real.

Because I didn't properly drop her class, it cost me six hundred dollars. The problem was that word got around the campus that I was a 'serious problem,' so every class I tried to take was full. The first person I vented to about this was Bella. It was things like that that made her want to be a lawmaker. Bella held her own too when things like that would occur in her classes. She'd chew her peers up and spit them out, then talk about the importance of representation so we as a people know what we are capable of. She also promoted unity when she saw a need to.

Roman and I had sex almost every day since we re-connected. That Thanksgiving break we had sex every single day until one day when I was too fatigued to give up the goods. With school, work and the stresses of being home, all I wanted to do when I got to Roman's was sleep. He'd get a little pissed off with me for wanting to be asleep all the time. But, he knew when I was in the mood it was some of the best- if not the best- cookie he'd ever had.

Bella was back in town for the weekend, so I went and spent time with her. Her favorite thing to make on a cold winter night was pasta. Her mom used to joke all the time saying how she had a big ol' pasta booty because that's all she ever ate. On one particular Friday night, she made spaghetti, and we bought a bottle of wine. I loved when she made spaghetti because she made the sweetness of the sugar blend perfectly well with sauce. I naturally got a big bowl of it, but just as fast as I gulped it down was as fast as I threw it back up. I tried to go into her kitchen to drink some water, thinking that it went down the wrong pipe but I couldn't hold any water down either. I fell to the ground, and Bella came running in.

When I finally came to, she asked me if I was pregnant.

"No, I don't think so. I don't feel funny," I said quickly.

"I don't know girl. Not holding anything down is usually a sign," she said.

Come to think of it, I hadn't had my period yet.

"Your nose does look a little big; I wasn't gonna say anything, but now it makes sense," Bella said.

"Damn, bitch- don't write me off just yet," I replied.

"Let's go get you a pregnancy test," she said.

"A pregnancy test," I thought. The thought never occurred to me. For some odd reason, I thought that I was gonna be someone who couldn't get pregnant after the first couple times we had sex with no condoms. I was so nervous. I didn't know what I would do if this was true.

We got into Bella's car and drove to the Walgreens at the end of her street. When we got inside, she told me to choose a two-pack pregnancy test so that I could double check. I was scared to take it at her house in case her mom found the wrapping in their trash can, so we drove to the McDonald's down the street, and I took the test in the bathroom. I ordered a coffee and fries while we waited for the results. Two minutes later, two lines popped up on the stick. That meant it was positive. I was in instant denial, so I took another one while we was there. I took two more when we came back to her house. They all read the same thing. Bella just looked at me waiting for me to snap back into reality. All I could think of was how much my shit wasn't together. I wasn't ready to be anybody's mother.

"Do you wanna call ya baby daddy?" Bella said, breaking the long, awkward silence.

"Uh, I don't know- I mean, I'm not sure what to tell him," I said.

"Tell him you're pregnant," Bella said.

"Well duh, I just mean I'm not sure if I want to be a mom right now," I said, "I can't even imagine what my mom would say."

"It's not anybody's decision but yours," Bella said, "things like this happen all the time. Whatever decision you make, I support you. If you make the decision not to keep it, I know a place where you can go so the procedure can be done as safely as possible."

All I can say back was, "Okay."

"You don't wanna go to a place like Planned Parenthood because they do it in the most traumatizing way possible and I heard it hurts, she said."

"Yea, let me think about what I wanna do; I'm gonna talk to him about it tonight," I said.

When I called Roman and told him the news, he didn't seem surprised. It was like he knew he slipped up. It didn't take him that long to pull up to Bella's house to get me. It's something about knowing that you're pregnant that makes all the symptoms pop up. Just like magic, certain scents were bothering me, I got really emotional, and I didn't really have an appetite. That night, we talked about the possibilities. I expressed to him clean off the bat that I didn't want to be a mother, but I didn't really believe in getting rid of a baby. He was on the same page as me; we both were in shock that I was actually carrying his child. I asked him if he'd ever gotten a girl pregnant; he said he had not.

"I never wanted a baby mama. I always said whoever I get pregnant, I was gonna marry," he said.

"Marriage?" I thought.

I guess I was supposed to be happy. Was that a proposal? I certainly didn't want to get married because of a baby.

"Do you love me?" I asked.

He quickly replied, "I got love for you, especially because you're pregnant with my child."

I didn't like that answer. I wanted to go home that night. My cousins were still living with us so, I had to sleep with my mom. My mom knew my period like clockwork, and for some reason that day she asked me if I was on. "Yes," I told her. I lied. I was scared. Luckily, I was spotting, so I would act like I was going to the bathroom to change a pad, then put the pad with a forced drop of blood on it in the trash. I could barely sleep at night. I could barely breathe. I didn't have an appetite during the day, so when I woke up during the nights, I would throw up acid. I didn't really want to be around Roman because of what he said, and I still hadn't made a decision.

For the next couple weeks, going to work every day, trying to finish up the semester, and taking the finals really took a toll on me. When I did begin to crave food, I wanted Chinese shrimp fried rice, Chinese fried chicken, and a shrimp egg-roll every day. When Roman picked me up from work, he made sure he had my food, or I'd burst into tears and go on and on about how he didn't care.

Every time I looked in the mirror, I saw how much my nose spread across my face. Through all the sickness I dealt with in just the few weeks since I knew I was pregnant, I began to bond with my baby. The idea of me and Roman being a family started to excite me more and more. When our winter break finally came, I built up the courage to tell him that I wanted to keep it. He came and picked me up from work as usual with my Chinese food. For some reason that made me feel like he was gonna be a great dad. On the way to his house, I told him that I was going to make a doctor's appointment. He was excited for the wrong reason. See, I was making one to see how far along I was and get the proper care. My mom worked for the school district so my insurance covered everything I would need.

"Cool- I'll be there with you," he said, "I'm glad you made that choice because I'm not ready to be a dad yet."

My heart fell in my lap. As I was scrambling over the words to say back, he continued.

"Plus, I don't know how I would have told Shelly."

Shelly was the ex that he swore he wasn't seeing again, so in my confusion, I yelled, "Why would it matter what she thinks anyway?"

"Well, I know this would've probably hurt her feelings, and I'm close with her family- I know they would've had a lot to say," he said.

I threw up all in his car. All I could muster up and say was, "Take me home." Along with the fear of what my mom, uncles, dad, and grandparents would say, my life not being together and the father of my child worrying about what his ex might think was enough for me to make that appointment to see Dr. Yaffa.

January 3, 2013, was the date set for life to be taken away from me. Roman called me every day to make sure I was going to go through with it.

"I'm just not ready to be a dad," he said. But I knew it had something to do with Shelly. I knew somewhere in between our rendezvouses he was seeing her.

During Christmas, I forced myself to get up as early as my little sisters did so no one would notice a change. We had dinner at my great aunt's, and she went on and on about how proud of me she was and how I made it through high school without any kids. That's when the guilt began. Bella would reassure me when I needed it that God understood, still loved me, and would forgive me. I kept repeating to myself that I was doing what was best. I didn't want to bring a child into this world whose daddy didn't want them. I took it a step further and thought about my birth. How'd my dad take the news? It must've been the same way because I can't remember a time where they were together. I didn't want to be judged by my family for having a baby so young. I didn't have things under control mentally, and I didn't want to bring a baby into that and raise it alone. New Year's came around, and I drank wine at my aunt's get together so I would seem normal. A half a cup, and I threw up all over the bathroom and passed out on the floor. My cousins, mom, and aunt had their phones out recording me teasing me about how much of a 'lightweight' I was.

January 3rd came sooner than I wished. It's like my child knew what I was about to do because the night before my termination was the sickest I'd ever been. I probably got a total of three minutes to sleep because of how much time I spent throwing up. Roman was outside my house at 6:30 am that next morning to take me to my appointment. We rode there silently. Bella had told me about this place. Dr. Yaffa was a private doctor who specialized in what I was looking for.

It was a small doctor's office. There was one couple, and the other two people were there because they'd gotten themselves into some shit. Listening to their very loud conversation put me in a lighter mood. They called my name to go back. They took my vitals and did a sonogram. I closed my eyes. I couldn't look at that little dot and fall in love in the middle of my appointment. The nurses were nice, trying to convince me that I was making a "smart decision." I was almost two months. They sent me back to the lobby, and I sat with Roman. He saw the fear in my eyes, but he wouldn't fix his mouth to tell me I didn't have to do it. I think he knew that's all he had to say, and I wouldn't have done it. His fear of hurting someone else was stronger than the love he had for something we created. My fear of making him mad was stronger than my physical capability to walk right out that door. He held my hand until they called me back for the actual procedure. I didn't know what to expect. They sat me on the hospital bed, and while they wrapped my arm in the IV, they talked normally to me about what I do for a living and my everyday life until I saw the back of my eyelids.

Then, I woke up. No one was in the room when I came to. My pants and underwear were neatly folded in the chair next to me, and I got up quickly in a panic. I was super dizzy, and when I noticed that they still had the tools that they used out, I began crying hysterically. I was in immediate regret. I didn't remember how I got to the room, but I found my way back to the lobby. As soon as I saw Roman,

I fell into his arms and kept crying loudly. The nurses told him to get me out of there. His only words of comfort were, "Damn, that shit must've been real." He offered to get me something to eat and to go back to his house to get some rest. But, I just wanted to go home. I hated him, and I hated myself for letting fear drive me to do something like that. I couldn't think of a single reason God would forgive me. I fought Him when everything inside me was telling me to give birth.

I slept for the rest of that day, and the day after that, and the day after that. In fact, sleep was the only thing that took away the hurt and the pain. So, sleeping is the only thing I did for a while. Regret became second nature. It took me some time to tell Jewel, partly because she wasn't an emotional supporter and she wasn't here physically to help me kill a bottle of whatever. Bella checked on me, but she could only hear so many 'it's okays' before that convinced her I was. When days got really bad for me emotionally, I isolated myself in frustration that no one could see past my forced smile and unassigned obligation to be there for everyone else but myself. I hated that Bella didn't force me to talk about my hurt but instead disregarded the fact that I was hurt so that I could be there for her. I didn't blame her because I knew it wasn't her job to force me to be vocal about my hurt and she too was facing challenges. So, she chose to fill herself up with whatever support I poured out. Somewhere in the mix of me being stoic, accepting, and loving her for who she was, I found comfort in knowing that I wasn't the only one who was going through something. I poured, and poured, and poured out what I called "support" or "being a good friend" for someone who was the image of resilience to me. I didn't realize I had nothing to pour, so I found myself drained. I blame intellectualization.

Happiness depends upon ourselves—Aristotle.

CHAPTER FOUR

Reaction Formation

/Reaction Formation/
A defense mechanism. The tendency of a repressed
wish or feeling to be expressed at a conscious level in a
contrasting form.

My termination made regret a big part of my character. I didn't have the desire to go back to school for the second semester. My mom wouldn't go for any of that dropping out shit, so every day I got dropped off at school, I would wait at least an hour and take the bus back home to crawl right back into bed. My cousins and aunts were still at my house during the day, and they did a great job of keeping that secret from my mom. An hour before her and my sisters came home, I would walk to Garvy's house-who lived only a few blocks away, smoke with him, then come back and go back to my bed. It all seemed like I had a long day at school and wanted to come home and go to sleep.

Mid- February, when the college kids still had school and the city district kids had mid-winter break, I went to Garvy's house to smoke early in the morning and ended up spending the entire day with him getting high and eating snacks we would get from the corner store at the end of his street. Sometimes, we would go to a park nearby that sat high up, so it had a nice view. Garvy knew I was "different," so it didn't concern him that I would sit on the grass as close to the middle of whatever piece of land we were on and meditate. I was secretly asking God for forgiveness and understanding. I knew that it had already been granted, but I needed to feel that for myself, so I could escape from the mental prison I put myself in.

One day, I came home early from "school" and forgot that my mom was gonna be home. I walked in, and my family was staring at my blood red eyes. They probably knew I was high. I quickly masked it as tiredness, and when my mom asked me why I was home so early, I told her that I kept falling asleep in class, so I just came home early. But, before I could rush to my bed, she asked me to pass her the mail that she quickly opened. I saw her face turn from a look of curiosity to figuring out the "evil" thing that I had done. You see, the private office had a confidentiality policy- so it didn't exactly state that I had an abortion, but I couldn't explain why a checkup cost nearly $3,000. That night I had to hear how evil I was, and if she knew she would've made me keep it. That didn't surprise me coming from her- and it did no more damage to our relationship than before. It made me want to rebel.

⌒∞⌒

In the '90s, it's safe to say that it was a lot safer to go places as a child with minimal supervision. Holdin and I took the money our grandfather gave us and walked to the corner store hand in hand, and got 2 bags of chips, a Little Hugs Juice, and some penny candies- all with a dollar. I was dying to tell Holdin what Uncle Norm was asking me to do, but I knew it would break the family apart. I didn't want to be face-to-face with him again that day, so as we started getting closer and closer to the house I stopped Holdin right in front of our cousin's house and told him I was gonna stay there until my mom came. I secretly regretted that too, because I knew it hurt my grandmother. She always thought that I'd rather be over there than at her house like I didn't like her or something, but I was too young and afraid to articulate the truth to her. I was afraid that she'd think I was lying. The next day though, I made my choice to go over there permanently.

Of course, Uncle Norm found me in the middle of one of me and Holdin's play dates and asked if I had my shit together yet. I said, "Yes" and went to the same room I was in the day before to try to hurry up and get it over with. It went down the same way. I went into the room; he closed the door and stood in front of it. I looked in the mirror and began slowly taking off my clothes. When they were all finally off, I heard the door creak open.

"Hold on, I'm still naked," I yelled, "I'm not done practicing."

"Ok, but you gotta hurry up Star; let me know if you need help," he replied.

I thought to myself about what kind of help I would need from him when I had all the magazines right next to me. Then I looked toward the door to make sure I still had my privacy, and I saw an eye looking through the crack at the bottom of the door. Then it dawned on me. I hadn't seen a single person he mentioned. There was no camera, and no examples or pictures of people he did this with before, no proof of him actually making my dreams come true.

"If he's so well connected, why does he still live with grandma?" I wondered.

I put my clothes on as fast as I could. He opened the door as I was doing so, asking me what I was doing. The wonder of how he knew I was "doing something" didn't dawn on me until I got out of there.

"I want to go home. Can I call my mom?" I asked.

"What you wanna go home for," he asked, "if you don't get this right your gonna be wasting all the money I put into this."

I didn't give a single fuck. I went past him out of there, and he kept yelling behind me that I was a "fast-ass little girl," "spoiled" and "selfish." I had no time to let anybody know that I was going over my cousin's house; I just ran right out the door. My mom never questioned why I always wanted to be there, so it didn't matter how much my grandmother huffed and puffed. I was safe there.

My mom never figured out that I didn't return to school that next semester. Her reaction to what I did was enough for me to go to Garvy's and smoke it away. I never told him about what happened, but he knew that I was in some type of pain and being with him is how I vented. Roman and I had agreed that this was a bit much for both of us and decided to fall back from each other for a while. I was beginning to believe that he felt just as guilty as I did because we still saw each other after all that happened and I questioned why we didn't keep the baby. Of course, that placed a large amount of guilt on my shoulders, and regret wasn't far away. I just couldn't bring myself to face something that I regretted.

I subconsciously put in place a plan to "heal" myself. When I ran out of "happy places" to daydream about I walked to Garvy's, and if Garvy wasn't home, I linked with Boss. If I wasn't with either of them, I was working. I was starting to engage more at my job because the people that worked there were actually funny. I started opening my eyes to how fine the brothers were that worked there. These were the type of guys I could have a friendship with. They brought out my tomboyish ways. When the boss wasn't looking, we'd play-fight, throw food, crack jokes, splash water on each other and go home. The job ended up being the place of repression, and I had gotten to a place where I could engage with the world again.

Bella was graduating that year with her bachelor's and was planning on moving out of town again. I was sad, but I knew she needed an escape from the things she was dealing with. I tried not to show how much I needed her presence when I was in an ok space mentally, but she knew it and would voice it. Of course, I followed up with the lies that I was gonna be okay. We did spend the remainder of her time together though; we even went to Puerto Rico with her sister and another friend. We had our legendary talks about God until four in the morning, watched our favorite movies, cut a couple of corners, and went to a few parties. We even ended up seeing one of the guys- Michael- a couple of times, and he saw how nice I looked outside of work. Everything was going on okay in life again.

My cousins- aka my sisters- Rose and Marie, were also a big part of my life that year. We formed our own little squad, including Marie's friend, Tina, and it helped me because me and my friends from high school had gone our separate ways. We still kept in contact, but there were no more squad moments like the old days. The days Marie had to work, it would just be me, Rose, and Tina. We named ourselves the Brown Skin Crew.

One night, the crew had one of our legendary Friday's on a Friday night and got so wasted. It didn't help that every time we went, we only had to buy our first drink- if that was before drinks were sent over to our table. We ran into me and Rose's male cousin- who swore he was our father. Of course, he made him and his friends sit at the table with us. He acted like no other guy was allowed to talk to us, but he had no issues trying to talk to our friends.

"Yea, let me check on you Ms. Star," he said.

I rolled my eyes.

"I'm glad to see you're drinking," he said.

"And why is that," I laughed.

"Last time I seen ol' boy he said he was getting ready to be a father," he said.

"Oh shit," I thought. I knew if nobody else was gonna kill me for being pregnant, he sure would've.

"Oh, I don't know what he talking about, maybe some other chick," I replied, "we aren't really seeing each other anymore."

"Oh, ok, good," he replied.

Whew! He believed it, and the heat was off me. We continued to get crazy drunk that night and our cousin had to bring us all home. We left Tina's car in the parking lot.

At seven o'clock that next morning, my cousin blew my phone up about three times. I ignored it because I had a huge hangover and I just wanted to sleep it off. When I finally got up around nine, I read a lengthy text from my cousin saying how he was sorry for asking me if I was pregnant. He told me he knew who Roman's baby mother was now and that he was glad I wasn't talking to Roman. He believed the girl Roman got pregnant was the most promiscuous girl in the city. I sat in denial a couple minutes after that, thinking of so many other possibilities. Maybe he had mistaken it for one of his other brothers.

"A ho?" I thought. Well, he did say Shelly left him twice for different guys- but damn, a baby? Maybe that's why he was so nervous when I got pregnant. I took a deep breath, texted him and asked him if he had a baby on the way. He didn't respond to me until nine that night and simply said, "Yea." There was no explanation, no "I'm sorry," no nothing. Moments after he told me yes, he posted a girl who was not Shelly, on his Instagram and announced that he was going to be a father and how important it was for him to take care of his "responsibilities." That was the last time we communicated with each other.

Going insane is an understatement. He damn near begged me to get rid of my baby, just to turn around- not even a full year later- and have another one with someone who had sex with 80 percent of our city. The only reason I could gather in my head was that she was freakier than me because she wasn't fucking with me in no other subject. Not even the group message going around saying how dumb he was for getting her pregnant and how everyone in the group message was a possible candidate for being the father made me feel better. It actually made me feel worse, and in the word of the great Eddie Griffin, "you don't fuck down- you fuck up." That made me extremely insecure. I didn't know what to do with my emotions. I felt dumb, dumber than I felt when Dame did what he did. I looked in the mirror and began to see all these flaws, lying to myself, telling myself that things were wrong with me. Instead of facing it, I pushed it back in my subconscious, where it was safe and I re-re-invented myself. His brothers and sister inboxed me on Facebook, apologizing to me for their brother. It was nice, but not enough. I had to feel better about myself by myself. My mind, heart, and spirit were tired.

The first act in re-inventing myself was responding to the inbox Michael sent me a week before on a Saturday night saying, "Where the party at?"

I replied a week later, asking him, "Where the party at?" Asking that on a Sunday was a clear indication that I wanted the party to be between him and me. He held a lot of weight in our city- low key- he wasn't the type of man I had in mind for the future, but to get something different you gotta do something different. I somehow put in my head that I would "conquer" my next relationship by being completely in control of when I hung with him and even when I talked to him. No more Mrs. Nice-Wannabe- Wifey Girl.

Bella put me on to a book called Why Men Love Bitches, and I thought that was the missing factor in my failed relationships. I mean, I was a bitch, but not in the beginning and not until they did something. Even then, it was short-lived. Then I went shopping. Since superficial trumps girls with brains, I had to become her to get what I wanted. I bought unnecessarily tight clothing to wear to work to highlight my figure. I began to go to as many parties as I could with a distant cousin who lived for the weekend. I drunk it away.

In my search for a good THOT outfit, I ran into Roman's sister. She was his sister from his father's side and didn't live with them. She had apologized again for her brother's actions, and I was vocal with her about him begging me to get rid of my baby. She told me the real on his situation. "I just can't believe he's marrying her," she expressed.

I tried so hard to keep a straight face. This was new information. "Married?" I said.

"Yea girl, he's only doing it because he's going to the army and when you're married you get more money," she said.

"Well he always told me he was gonna marry the person he got pregnant," I said, "I guess he didn't want it to be me."

"Girl she's giving him hell. He didn't want her to have her's either, but he never showed up to her appointment to get it done. Now she says she's keeping it. That's what he gets though because she's his karma," she said.

All I could do was focus on not looking so pressed.

"Well, I hope he get what he deserves," I replied.

I couldn't wait to get home and cry my eyes out. Everything was falling apart around me, including my family. Two of my younger female cousins confessed to a disturbing claim that Holdin had sexually abused them. They also claimed that my little sister was a victim and before you knew it, we were all separated. All I could think about were the things that I went through in that house, so it wasn't hard to believe. In the same breath, I was always with Holdin around the ages that they claim it happened and I always remember all of the kids playing "house" and "wedding." Like all curious kids do in the stages of development, we got caught being "fresh." Of course, Aheem had a field day with that, but my sister said for her it wasn't true. We didn't speak to them for a while, but it wasn't long before we were talking again.

My mom had bought a new house down the street from Bella. We were both hyped. I wish we could've lived over here before she went to college though because we still had limited time to see each other. When she went away at the end of that summer, Michael became my ultimate scapegoat. With the tight clothes I bought drawing more attention to my assets, Michael couldn't help but to ask me to hang out after work one day. Of course, I agreed as planned. We had spent some of the summer texting. I stuck to what I said and let him be the first person to text me every time we talked, that let me know that he was interested. He was the type of guy who expected to be sweated, and everyone expected for someone to sweat him. Although I waited by my phone for a text from him, I NEVER reached out to him first. I even took a couple hours to respond. He was not about to add me to the list of girls that was all over him. He even said to me once we hung out for the first time, that "he gotta catch me while he can" because I never texted back. I thought that maybe we was just gonna smoke and talk or something, but he started driving toward the other side of town. My prude ass asked if he was bringing me back home later that night- and he said no. I lit another blunt to kill my anxiety.

When we got to his house, I stayed as far away from him as possible. Then, it was time for bed, and after a normal smoke session. I didn't bring anything to change into, so he gave me a t-shirt and some basketball shorts. He did a pretty good job of keeping his hands to himself that night until he couldn't take it anymore. He scooted closer to me and started touching me. Immediately, I started crying. In my head, I knew for sure he was gonna be on the next thing running taking me back home. To my surprise, he backed off and asked me what was wrong. I tried to suck up my tears and talk. While I was trying to get my shit together, he began to imitate me and sob with me. My crying turned into laughter. "

What are you doing?" I said in between chuckles.

"You making me feel like a predator," he said and continued to fake sob.

I wiped my tears away and laughed louder. "I just don't think this is the right moment," I said. He respected it, and we continued life as usual. I still had in my head that he still wouldn't want to hang out with me after that, but we still texted, and we still acted normally at work.

I loved my new house. I decorated my room in the exact way that expressed me. Boss liked to go to the Sound Garden as much as I did. That's where they had almost any music records from the 50's and 60's. He took me there so I could get my Beatles calendar and any other gear I needed for my room. He became a big part of this healing process I called myself going through.

Aheem was the type of guy that was jealous of his woman showing any signs that she didn't need him. My mom allowed him to come along to our new house too and of course, they argued per usual. He would find new and creative ways to express his anger. Within the first few weeks of us moving in, he got mad one night, and we woke up to no hot water and lights cut off manually. He was that good with his hands but never used them for a good purpose. He had promised my mom that he would re-do the things she wanted done in our house so we could save some money, but he held that over her head. He would start a project but take months to finish it just so he could have an excuse to act a fool and be able to come back. Of course, me voicing my opinion would start an argument between her and me and the negative energy would transfer from him to me and I would have to leave to gain some sanity.

That's the night me and Michael had our first sexual encounter. He just so happened to have texted me to hang out- the same night Aheem started his shit. I had told him that I wanted to spend the night and I packed an overnight bag. We hung out first, like we normally would, and I so high to hide my frustration, my sexual drive went up. I expressed that to him, and he tried to fight how excited he was that I had decided to give it up. He started off slowly, in case I had another panic attack, but that night I felt like Rhianna in one of her videos, smoking weed and ready to get busy. I wanted to fuck the stress away. I let him take all my clothes off as I stared intensely into his eyes. He would become the first guy to have gotten me completely naked to have sex and the first guy to say that we fucked each other. I came, releasing the stress along with it. I felt so relieved and rejuvenated, fucking him became a habit. I didn't want him to be my man though. I learned that putting expectations on a man only leads to disappointment, so I took our situation for what it was. It was like I was fucking my best friend.

Between him and Boss, I had created the perfect situation. Boss' and my relationship became a Jada and Pac relationship- but that's all it was. We could vibe emotionally, but he was not my Will Smith. Michael and I had friendship- but not an emotional one. It was more like us cracking jokes and smoking weed like regular homies; sometimes I would watch him play his PlayStation and played him in a game or two. He was extremely competitive, so I would get annoyed and quit. I would make him watch The Braxton Family Values so much that he was looking forward to Thursday nights. Beyonce was blessing us with HBO specials, and I made him watch all of those. Somewhere in between that, we had sex.

Bella was living it up in college, and I would keep her updated via text, or we would have one of our talks by phone. However, my daily routine was going to work, hanging out with Boss, and vibing to all the old music I listened to. I would vent to him about my mom, and we smoked until Michael was ready to go in the house. I'd smoke a couple more times with Michael, and we hung out and had sex. I was so invested in my daily situation that every time I went to the mall, I'd buy some sort of lingerie or lacy panties to wear over to Michael's. Our sexcapades gave me such quick thrills that I longed for them and became more creative with our sex life. I consumed so much water and raw cranberry juice you'd think I was dieting. I kept my flower extra tight and juicy; Roman would gag over the freak I became. I even re-enrolled in school. We managed to keep our rendezvous secret for a whole year and a half before people at our job started putting two and two together. They started questioning why he was worried about if I ate or not.

Nobody was really worried about what me and Michael had going on at that job until two of the most hateful girls came to the job. I'm just gonna call them Frick and Frack. Of course, no one's true colors are shown off rip; they played nice at first. So nice, that at one point I would consider them friends. I was never vocal to anyone other than Bella about my situation with Michael, but since they pressed me about it, I confirmed with the two ladies that me and Michael were involved. They also taught me the true meaning of jealousy. They loved me, or the idea of me. From the outside looking in, I looked like the typical superficial girl who looked nice and cared about looking pretty. It always helps to have a pretty girl on your team. What they hated was that they learned I was so much more than that once they got to know me. The things I told them about me "upgrading" what I wore to attract attention turned into rumors of me having a fake butt and Michael giving me the money to do it. Luckily, Michael wasn't with all that drama, so he shut those rumors down quickly. Then they tried to befriend him and tell him things about me. When he and I would hang out privately, he expressed to me how mad he was that I even confided in them. I took it in a whole other way than what he actually meant. I thought maybe he was trying to keep me a secret, and that's the real reason why he was mad. He knew that everything they were saying was a lie, but all the drama made him distant.

It got worse when we got a new kid, Jordan, who came to the job and showed interest in me. Frick and Frack cried wolf to one of my bosses, and we ended up having a conversation to "dead the beef." Forgiving me- understanding that jealousy played a factor, accepted their apologies and re-kindled our "friendship." Needless to say, it was an act of insanity. I did what I thought was smart and gave them an inch. I didn't go to their houses like I used to and we didn't hang out anywhere else outside the job. I ended up befriending Jamie, another young lady at the job, who kept to herself. I needed to get back to that character.

Of course, Frick and Frack got jealous and started a rumor that I was trying to "steal" Jordan from her. The gag is, her and Jordan never liked each other. They were just friends, and I was still all about Michael. I had to go to the lengths of asking Jordan if he could call me while I was at Michael's, just to prove to Michael that the things they were saying weren't true. I decided to scrap the friendship for good with Frick and Frack because the good thing that I built was falling apart. We were now at war. By this time, everyone at the job knew that Frick and Frack started all this bullshit with me and now added Jamie so the rumors no longer worked.

What they did was build an army with the new faces that constantly came to the job, so now a whole group of females didn't like me before they even met me. All they saw was a superficial chick who thought she was all that. They would purposely do things so that I wouldn't be able to do my job properly.

We all had to stand in a tray line together, so the dirty-ass looks lasted for eight hours a day. They constantly would talk shit to one another, and it was worse when Jamie wasn't there to back me up. Jordan was the only one who would sit and talk with me when Jamie didn't come. Michael had switched off that shift, and word got back to him that I was eating lunch with Jordan and I started seeing him less and less. I was on the verge of losing my mind. I started engaging in the shit-talk, except mine would be a lot more explosive, turning the attention on me like I was the aggressor. I would get written up and suspended, but I didn't care. I wasn't new to being looked at as the aggressor, and I was tired. It had gotten to a point where I was plotting on how I was gonna fuck these bitches up for all the shit they created in my life. I was so focused on seeking revenge that I hadn't even noticed that Michael was gone from our job for good. I saw him a couple times after that, but then one of my cousins saw him at a bar getting back with his ex- or who looked to be- and I never answered a text or call from him again. Every day of

199

my life at work was full of drama, so I didn't put up a fight trying to explain to him or get him back. I didn't even want an explanation from him on why he was out doing what he was doing. Bella had come home to deal with things going on in her family so any time I saw her, I had no time to vent about it

Somehow, the devil got that piece of information to Frick and Frack's ears and when they thought that they had "won," all hell broke loose. EVERY SINGLE DAY I came to the job with a mission to whoop ass. I even called my crazy-ass cousin who thought she could swing by my job, whoop ass, then make it to her job on time. But, of course, it's no fun when the rabbit got the gun. All of a sudden, Frick and Frack would call into work, switch days, or stay as close to the boss as possible to avoid my wrath. Even Jamie had enough; the same gang of girls was giving her hell too, and when you realize you can't beat someone, you join them. One by one, they started switching to the other side. Jamie would speak, but I was on some keep that same energy shit.

In the middle of my bullshit Sunday morning, I got a phone call from my mom- crying. My mother didn't usually cry, in fact, the only time I saw her shed a tear was when my grand-mother passed away. She had told me that my little cousin passed away. I dropped the phone and burst into tears. She was Mia's age, and they were damn near like sisters. My heart mainly broke for her. Our little cousin was Mia's scapegoat from all her pain. What's even sadder was that the night before, she was experiencing some sort of "period cramps," as she described to her mom. She was admitted in the hospital because of all the pain. She was healthy; she was the captain on the basketball team at her high school, and she exercised daily. But, when she checked in, she never checked out. I was starting to think that's how my family was gonna leave this place- unexpectedly.

The bitch caught me on a bad day. A newbie came and was under Frick and Frack's spell. I was newly back to work from my cousin's funeral, and this bitch I never had dialogue with couldn't keep my name out her throat. I finally yelled, "Fuck it," and started going the fuck off. See, Frick and Frack got smart and decided to level up and take the CNA classes they had available for anyone who wanted to bid out, so this new bitch had no one to save her. They weren't gonna do anything anyway. The argument got so heated that Jordan had moved from his spot in the line to try and calm me down. Like any other wannabe tuff person, as soon as she saw someone holding me back, she got even more hype and shot a plate at me. I pushed past Jordan and grabbed a bucket of bowls and used her head as target practice. She was pregnant, so I was being mindful as far as I was concerned. My boss, the meanest one there, stood up for me because she witnessed all the shit they put me through, and she knew my cousin just passed away. I thought I had a fighting chance to keep my job, but her mom was a union rep at our job, so that was an automatic termination. The only people who kept in contact with me were Jordan, Jamie and one of Michael's friends, Thomas. Turns out Frick had no one else to terrorize, so she leaked a photo of Frack's drawers around the building.

Some people's evil doings will create a worse prison than anybody can wish on them- all because of insecurities. I, for one, wished I could've witnessed the madness, but in order to be humbled by your own situation sometimes, it's best not to see karma happen to somebody but be happy with just knowing. Jordan tried to come to my rescue and be my man. I entertained it for a while thinking that because he was so nice and attentive, that he might be a good one. After a while, I had to be honest with myself. I didn't really like him, and I didn't have to force myself to try and like him just because he was nice and did what a man was supposed to do. Plus, I felt dirty entertaining it, knowing all the things I went through trying to prove that I didn't like him in the first place. It was time to just let myself hit rock bottom.

It was a struggle trying to get another job. It was a whole month since I got fired and I still had the obligation to pay everyone's phone bill. I had asked my grandmother for some money to cover this month, but the phone bill was about to be due again, and there was only so many extensions I could ask for. I knew my cousin was always a part of some type of get rich quick scheme, so I reached out to her for some help. Her brother just so happened to inquire about a way we could get some quick cash. He said he knew a way where money could appear on your account through the computer and all he needed was my bank information. With no hesitation or thinking it through, I had agreed. Anybody with a brain would have looked at that as a red flag, but I was so thirsty for money I handed the info over. I guess I thought that because he was kind of like family that he wouldn't do anything grimy. But, there I was, putting an expectation on a man again.

The day everything was supposed to happen, my intuition was going crazy. I never had a stronger bad feeling about something. I called my cousin Marie, and she barked on me instantly and told me to call 'my bank' before he could do anything and stop any transactions. My bank called me before I can even call them; they had it set up to where they knew how much money I usually spent in a day. If it went over that, they asked if it was me doing the spending. I lied and told them that I was trying to make a transaction and it said insufficient funds, so that was the reason for my call. They made sure to let me know before I got off the phone that whoever had my account illegally cashed out in

Walmart, Target, Destiny, USA YESTERDAY and $4,000 had been taken out of my MOTHER'S account to cover the cost because ours were joined and I didn't have any money in my account.

She might as well put death on the phone to tell me to say my last words. The first thing I did was panic and tried to come up with a good enough lie to explain $4,000 missing. Next, I called my cousin, whose brother it was that did the whole thing. I didn't think she would be equally pissed. I actually thought she might have known all along, but she came up with the suggestion to go to the police. Our dumb asses should've known in the first place that this was a scam. For some reason, I thought that going to the police made it easier to confess to my mom. A BIG-ASS WRONG. She flipped, rightfully so, and told me I had one month to pay her back or I could see my ass out of her house. That was more than fair. At first, I blamed her for putting so much pressure on me to maintain the phone bill even though she knew I didn't have a job. I had resentment towards her because Mia was well over age to find a job and pay her own phone bill. Aheem never worked a day in his life. This right here though was a new low for me. I could make a long list of faults- especially the fact that I had no one to help or to even offer help, but I realized how out of character I'd been acting.

I became regretful again. I was in deeper depression than I was before. I completely isolated myself from everybody, even Boss, who I would make an exception for in any other case. For three weeks straight, I didn't even want to be up. Every time I got up, I forced myself back to sleep. I did that by sitting very still and zoning out like a daydream to my own little world. I was dead broke and owed $4,000 to my mom and had to figure out a way to pay the phone bill. I was single and lonely, and because I never properly took time to heal from any situation I'd been through, the buildup of hurt was overwhelming.

I was always moving too fast. After my three-week hiatus, I went on for another few weeks and started a diary. Instead of forcing myself to sleep I wrote down how I was feeling. I slowly started back listening to my Sam Cooke and Jackie Wilson, and while Sam sang a Change is Gonna Come, it pushed me back into the arms of God. I locked myself in my room during the day, writing poems. I even taught myself how to play the guitar. At night, when I knew for sure that everyone was sleeping, I locked myself in the bathroom and took long showers. I prayed to God. I realized that I was living my life contrary to what I believed in to get what I really wanted.

The prayers went from me being too shameful to ask for forgiveness because I consciously made bad choices to fill a void, to talking and having full-blown conversations with God. I finally built up the confidence to look for jobs. I remember my pastor saying in church one day that God wants us to be so comfortable with Him that we treat Him and come to Him like we would our earthly father, brother, or friend. He also said not to be afraid to express our anger if we're upset with our misunderstanding. I kept that in mind as I was rebuilding my relationship with Him. If you were a fly on my bathroom wall, you would have thought I was going crazy. If you were a bystander listening from outside the bathroom, you would have thought I was either on the phone or someone was in the bathroom with me. I really talked to God. I was starting to get angry about not finding a job and my mom being down my throat. Stress was on the rise.

The night before I found a job, I was so frustrated by unanswered prayers that I couldn't hold back anymore. I yelled and screamed at God, expressing how bad I needed a breakthrough. I told him how mad I was because I didn't understand why I was going through so much hell and how the people who hurt me seemed like their lives were going perfectly fine. I let out every evil thought, every "why me" I could think of and cried until I fell asleep. The very next day, I got a call from UPS for a seasonal position. It wasn't exactly the job I hoped for, but it was something. I could at least start paying my mother back. Getting that blessing the next day made me understand God a little bit better. I understood that he wants us to be completely dependent on Him. Once I put my expectations on Him, my life changed. I learned that all my life I expected good things to just happen to me because I was a good person. I thought because my intentions were good for everything I involved myself in that even a bad decision would turn good. I was sadly mistaken. There's power in pain- yes! But a good heart only gets you God's mercy. At some point, you have to start taking responsibility for your actions. I put my expectations on things and people who couldn't make me happy, or have the power to change my life in positive ways. Being my authentic self was good enough for God. I also realized that because I was good enough for God's blessings by being myself, I didn't have to alter who I was to get someone to approve of me. I was already approved by the Most High.

This piece of understanding allowed me to pick myself up every day and work as hard as I could in those UPS trucks. It didn't completely take my hurt away, but understanding God that much more opened the door for me to not give up on my happiness; I started to crave more understanding. I wanted to understand the purpose of my pain, why did God allow certain things to happen to me.

Awareness is the greatest agent for change –Eckhart Tolle

CHAPTER FIVE

Awareness

Awareness
Knowledge or perception of a situation or fact.
The proof of spiritual maturity is not how pure you are
but awareness of your impurity. That very awareness
opens the door to grace- Philip Yancey.

I was well aware. The more time I spent with myself, the more freely I thought. It started to make sense the importance of Jesus Christ- or Yeshua as I now called him. He loved us so much that he took the time to identify with the mortal being to understand the challenges we go through, the things that we put ourselves through due to lack of understanding and insecurities. Yeshua is so important because now we have the will to live freely knowing that God understands our hearts. Once we fully grasp that, it's our job to live life as righteously as we possibly can in our own skin, being mindful that nothing can separate us from his love. The only sin or prison we put ourselves in is when we believe the lie that the things we do by human nature are so unpleasing to God that he won't love us anymore and send us to Hell. We stress over things that we feel are wrong so much that we forget to grow from them. In all actuality, the things WE ARE TOLD are wrong aren't wrong at all- it's just a man's philosophy. Our entire lives are lived accordingly to how someone feels- and not what God actually said. We are born innately knowing right from wrong. No one had to tell us that it's wrong to kill someone but when someone chooses it, it then becomes sin. Why? Because vengeance does not belong to us. How can it? We don't even fully understand life.

I freed myself from that prison. I stopped telling myself the lie that if I do something socially wrong, because of my perception, that I won't be favored by God. I let man tell me something that God did not say, and because of that, I imprisoned myself. I isolated myself. That was the case no more. I was starting to take responsibility for how I felt, and what I chose to do with those feelings. I chose to believe that I am human and there was a purpose for the things I went through. There was a reason for the things I went through. There was an awareness of self because of the choices I made. This all made me better, and I appreciated God as a parent for that.

As it got closer to the end of the seasonal position for UPS, I got really nervous because I didn't think I was gonna find another job. To my surprise, a week after my position was expired I got a phone call from TWO places willing to hire me. One was a position at 7- Eleven down the street from where I lived, and the second position was a special ed TA (teacher's assistant) at a middle school down the street from my house. I was lucky to land that job because of the college credits I already had; I felt so blessed. I was still in debt to my mom, and I still had to catch up on the phone bill. I decided to work both jobs. It worked out perfectly because after I got done at the school district job I was able to do the 7-Eleven job right after. It took up my entire day, but I was cool with it. Working from seven in the morning to ten at night was another form of a defense mechanism. I was still in denial about my healing process. Working all day took my mind of the painful things that happened because it took the focus off me.

Working at the school district though, turned out to be an unexpected blessing. The school system had changed a lot since I was in grade school, and everything they used was digital. When I got my assignment to work with a sixth-grade boy with several mental and health issues, I was nervous. I expected to see something like a 'bubble boy' from the way they described his needs to me. I read his IEP, which stands for individual educational plan, and it painted him out to be a complete nightmare. They told me that he ran his other one-on-ones off. They warned me of spitting, kicking, biting, running off, stubbornness, manipulation, and irrationalism. On top of that, they didn't have any record of him doing work- ever. The only way to keep him quiet was to let him sleep or play video games. Oh- and he didn't like to write. I just knew I wasn't gonna last long.

The first day I met him, he spat in the vice principal's hair twice and ran off. Luckily, I worked with an awesome teacher; otherwise, I wouldn't have returned the next day. The teacher I worked with advised me just to make sure he was not hurting himself and that he was occupied. He said he'd take care of everything else. I was thankful for him being so mindful because I really needed this job. Most people who have somewhat of authority over others are usually impossible to work with or don't care if your job is too difficult.

For two weeks straight, this little guy gave me a run for my money. When I tried to get him to do work, he'd start acting like a five-year-old and start throwing major fits. I was beginning to get stressed out again. The third week of working with him, I decided that I was gonna do everything in my power to keep him calm so I wouldn't be stressed out. I paid attention to the things that set him off so when it came time to cross that bridge, I bargained with him. I told him if he did what I asked him to do, I'd give him the last ten minutes of class to play any game he'd like. To my surprise, he complied. It started off with him doing one digital content program a day and progressed to all. He still didn't like to write because of bad penmanship, so I was trying to figure out a strategy for that too. I still had issues with his unpredictable behavior. After a while, he started to open up to me a little bit about himself. Once he realized that he couldn't run me off, he told me of his favorite things to do outside of school. He had a soccer game coming up that he wanted me to go to. At first, I wasn't gonna go, but then I thought about all the times I wanted people to see me past what others had to say and bear with me through the bullshit.

His game was only a block away from where I lived, so I took my little sister with me. When he saw me, he ran off the field in the middle of the game and ran up to me like I was his favorite celebrity. That warmed my heart so much. His parents ended up thanking me for actually showing up to one of his games. They knew how difficult he was in school, and me still showing up for him showed how much I actually cared. From that small act of endearment, he and I built a great relationship. The principals were impressed by how much his scores and behavior had improved in such a short time. Of course, they didn't thank me initially, but then the teacher I worked with stood up for me and told them that he had nothing to with his growth.

The teacher's act of endearment allowed us to build a close relationship also. Our relationship wasn't exactly ideal for people who worked there- because we were completely opposite. I was a woman. He was a man. I was black, and he was white. It surprised me as I realized the older I got how much race mattered to some people like we were living in the '60s. They hated the fact that he gave me so much credit. Because of him, I held weight around the school. The icing on the cake was how much Sam's parents came up to the school to thank me for actually building a relationship with their pale-skinned, red-haired, blue-eyed boy unlike anyone else there. I actually overheard fellow staff members talking shit saying that I thought I was the second coming of Jesus. Thankfully, I understood that how people viewed me had nothing to do with me, but was instead, a reflection of their insecurities. Otherwise, they would have cared less about what I was doing. Thinking that I thought of myself as a higher power in a negative way showed that the staff members themselves couldn't see how they could effectively influence a student as well as I did.

Working there also made me realize why representation mattered so much. In Sam's social studies class, they were watching the story of Ruby Bridges. I hadn't seen that movie since I was a young girl, and this time around I noticed something that I hadn't before. When Ruby Bridges was young and going through the difficulties of being the first black person to learn among white kids, a psychiatrist studied her to analyze how she was handling the stresses of the situation mentally. He noticed that when she drew pictures of herself and her peers she drew the images of the white children with faces and herself without a face. When he inquired about why she was doing that, he discovered that she viewed white people as superior beings because everything around her and what she was going through supported that.

That made me notice how unaware the African-American community was about the heroes that come from their same background. I started paying more attention to the other children in my class because of that. I took the liberty to build relationships with them the same way I built one with Sam. It shocked me to know that my life story didn't have shit on theirs. One little girl I got to know shared with me the things she had to deal with when she got home. I couldn't imagine being twelve years old with a mother on drugs, 4 of my 6 siblings dead and a depressed father. When she went home, she was no longer a little girl. She was the woman of the house. She had to look after her sibling that was still alive and make sure her father didn't forget to feed them. It was clear to me why she acted out so bad at school. No, it wasn't because of her label "special ed," it was because that's the only place she got to be a kid.

I learned why another young girl used to come to school and pee on herself. Of course, at first, I thought it was gross, and she just wasn't properly taught to take care of herself, but then I found out that she was raped by her older sibling and she was having nightmares. I also found out that peeing was used as a defense because no one would want to pursue her if she smelled. Like the common black family, being mentally ill isn't normalized, so she never expressed to her parents how she was feeling and what was going on. Every day, she would pee her pants before going home because she feared what was going to happen. She didn't want me to tell because she was afraid of getting in trouble with her parents because they hated when this happened. I didn't do what my job required of me to do right away because all I wanted to do was weep for her. I could identify with her on a level of trying to express something to your superheroes and them not understanding you or not willing to take responsibility.

I talked it over with one of my good friends I met at work that next day, and she assisted me in telling the proper authorities. They reassured me that things like that would be confidential, but when the little girl found out that someone told her parents she was pissed at me. I tried to act like I didn't know who told, but she knew that the only person she confided in about that situation was me. I had broken her trust. I beat myself up a couple days over it, but I knew

I helped save her life. Thankfully, her parents didn't get mad that she had told me. They actually appreciated the awareness. They got her some counseling, and she didn't have to worry about her older brother attacking her anymore.

She made me think about the meaning of my own life and purpose. I went through so much pain and stress my whole life because I didn't have anyone to talk to. I wanted to show her that even though she experienced such bad things, her resilience and bravery to speak up would show people that it will get better and they are not alone.

Me and Bella weren't as close as we once were because of my isolation, but I still kept her updated on my life as far as what I was into physically. Once I realized how I helped that little girl, I wanted to be more vocal with my own depression. She suggested I go to Vera House to really deal with the things I went through with my uncle. I agreed. I learned from my experience there that the spacing out to daydream thing was called depersonalization. Depersonalization is a mental disorder in which the person has persistent or recurrent feelings of derealization. It's described as feeling disconnected or detached from one's self. I stopped going after someone confirmed to me that what I was going through was an actual disorder and not pure craziness. I suddenly had this strong urge just to be free and live the best life I could regardless of what anybody had to say.

New Year's was coming up, and another good thing about working for the school district was the amount of paid time off we got. I wanted to get dressed up and go out of town; I didn't want to be anywhere local that year. I asked Bella if she wanted to go with me and she told me some excuse I couldn't remember. I had no one else to go with. Jewel and I had completely stopped talking a while back because I didn't get her a ticket to see one of her favorite artists. I didn't really fight for our relationship because of the pettiness of it all. Real friends don't fall off because of something so simple. We weren't beefing though; we just went our separate ways.

I didn't let any of that stop me though.

I remembered that Thomas lived in New York City. He and I kept in contact, and unlike a female, he didn't care how long it had been since we actually hung out. He was with the idea, and I wasted no time getting my bus ticket. It saved me a lot of money on a hotel too. I never traveled anywhere alone, and although New York City was only four hours away, I was still nervous. I made sure I downloaded all the music I loved, my belly was full and my bladder empty, so I could just get on the bus and fall asleep. I was lucky enough to have a seat to myself until the first stop in the next city. I was sitting to myself praying that no one weird sat next to me. I just wanted to continue to have a peaceful ride.

This old white guy that looked to be about 60-65 sat right next to me. At first, I was a bit uncomfortable. My discomfort led me to put my headphones on and blast the music so loud so that I wouldn't have to speak to him. But, him sitting next to me turned out to be one of the greatest experiences of my life. I wasn't completely rude though; I played a song that he might be able to identify with: La Vie En Rose by Louis Armstrong. Halfway through his trumpet solo, the old man tapped me on the shoulder. I thought he was going to ask me to turn my music down, but when I took my earbuds out he said, "Is that Louis Armstrong?"

I quickly replied with a "yes," and smiled.

"Oh wow- I didn't know someone like you would listen to that," he said.

I knew he was referring to my youth.

"That's one of my favorite love songs," he added.

"Mine too," I said.

"Yeah. What else do ya' know?" he asked.

"Well, I can bet you we both have another favorite love song," I said.

"Ok, let me have it," he said.

I gave him the other, and I played Happy Together, by the Turtles. He looked at me in shock.

"What do you know about the Turtles?" he said.

I knew he was referring to my youth and color when he said that.

"More than you'd know," I chuckled.

For the rest of the trip to New York City, we sat there together and listened to the downloaded albums on my phone. I played The Beatles', *Sergeant Pepper's*, The Turtles, Sam Cooke's *Portrait of a Legend*, The Kinks', *Face to Face*, Jackie Robinson's, *He's So Fine*, and Smokey Robinson and the Miracles.

I dreaded going back home. In the city, I felt so free. I dressed how I wanted, even if I was going somewhere simple. I listened to whatever music I wanted. I talked to God freely. I wore my hair how I wanted. I was an entire mood out there. Knowing I had to go back to act and do as others said had me frustrated. When Thomas walked me to my bus terminal, I started to cry. You'd think I just got a phone call that someone passed away the way I cried. I had to start doing something to free myself; prayer without works was dead. I had gotten back to a place where I could have my deep conversations with God, but I realized another thing about expectation. When I was praying for a job, I didn't ask for financial freedom. When I was praying to understand, I didn't pray for growth. I prayed for healing but never faced anything I went through. I prayed just enough to be ok enough to maneuver through everyday life but not enough to actually be alright. I didn't practice loving myself in real life. I still didn't forgive myself or others. I just expected all of that to come with it.

My first attempt at living my life as free as possible was fixing whatever was going on between me and Bella. I liked the idea of traveling more often. I liked the sense of freeness I felt with when I was away. It beat depersonalizing any day. I asked her if she would want to spend my birthday with me in Mexico. She was also doing something for her birthday- like every other year- and of course, I was with it. So, I gave her the money. I was trying to be away as much as possible. But, she wasn't able to join me on my trip. I, again, didn't let that stop me from going on mine; I invited (Jamie) to go with me. She had never been out of the country before and our birthdays were two days apart.

As it got closer to Bella's birthday, she decided to change her mind about the whole thing. She had rather take a vacation after she graduated that year. I was fine with that; I decided to go visit my grandfather with my dad and surprise him that year. I had no idea Bella would feel some type of way because of that. She texted me out of nowhere when I got back and said that we needed to talk. We didn't even get a chance to talk face to face. When I asked her "what about," she had revealed to me that she has been feeling a type of way since 2014 in a long, detailed text message. I didn't reply until the next day because the first line threw me off because the year was now 2017. And I just gave her money for another trip to celebrate her. For the past three years, we'd been on trips, parties, and the amount and depth of our conversations had me thinking that we were alright, and would always be. She said it had to do with my isolation and how during one particular time in her life I picked the wrong time to isolate in her eyes. When I responded, I actually took responsibility for my action of isolation. I also explained to her that at the time how I was depressed and I expected her to understand, being that she was my biggest cheerleader for me to do something about my mental health. I was honest with her about how drained and overwhelmed I felt at that time, and I couldn't clearly deal with anyone else's problems but my own. She always said, "You can't help anybody until you help yourself," and now all of a sudden, she couldn't understand that and called me a "bad friend," saying that by her asking for my comfort shouldn't be looked at as baggage.

She was right, but still missed the part that I too was drowning. I emotionally could not be there for anyone else, not out of spite or because I thought she was dependent on me, but because I didn't deal with what was going on with me, my mind demanded rest. Though all of that was going on, I was there for every situation she had been through, even the one she was talking about, up until I had nothing else to pour. She didn't want to understand anything I was, so I ended it by saying, "Sorry that I couldn't be the friend you needed me to be," and we never spoke again.

I never fought to rebuild that relationship, no matter how much I wanted to because my pride wouldn't let me after I saw her thank the same people who were never there for her and actually did some pretty devious things to her. That right there hurt me. I wasn't angry at all; anger to me is when a random person judges your character without knowing who you are. But, when you have had an intimate relationship with someone, and they judge your character, knowing what they know- it hurts. It's almost like going through a break-up. Just like that, ten years of friendship went down the drain. From that point on, I was on some 'if you're not already my friend we're not becoming friends' shit.

I thought I knew what healing looked like. But, once the failed attempt at making sure me and Bella's friendship was solid, I craved for another getaway alone. I did have fun with (Jamie) on my birthday trip, but my mind was somewhere else. Things at home between my mom and Aheem got worse and worse. One week, he got mad at my mom and poured white paint all on her new furniture, cut off the hot water so we wouldn't be able to take a warm shower, and left. It didn't stop there. He would take off cabinets, take off the siding on our house, and do his legendary all-night long rants.

One night, Sady ran up the stairs in somewhat of a panic waking me and Mia up because he had pushed my mom. Half dead, me and Mia hopped up and damn near skipped all of the steps so we could get to him- and we all jumped on him at once. We stopped once we realized we were getting the best of him. He left for a couple days, and my mom let him come back, like always. A few weeks after that, he got so high and drunk that he burst out in a panic thinking my mom had another man in her room. Mia and I woke up to Sady standing outside my mom's door, begging her dad to let her out. He had a dresser up against my mom's door so she wouldn't get out. He kept saying he saw somebody jump out her window and many more insane things. He eventually stopped around six that morning when his high came down. My sisters and I had never been so happy about a Saturday ever in our lives. Our eyes were bloodshot because we stayed up the whole time making sure my mom was okay since she insisted that we shouldn't call the police. We slept for the rest of that day. He asked if we could have a "family" meeting about his actions. I could care less, but my sisters saw that as an opportunity to get how they was feeling off their chest and wanted me there for support. They had always vented to me how they really felt about their father and how our mom was so insensitive to our feelings.

I remember when we actually tried to come to her and be open with how we felt and she couldn't seem to wrap her head around the fact that it had been affecting us. My sisters confessed that they were scared to date because they didn't want a man like their father. On top of that, he didn't have a relationship with them. He was literally only there for whatever reason my mom wanted him there. It was made pretty clear that our lives would be saner without him. She would tell us that we should learn from her, but she didn't get that it was indeed what we were doing. I voiced to her that she was basically teaching us that we should put up with the things he did, for whatever reasons. We had no idea from her or anybody else in our family what a stable relationship looked like. She didn't get the resentment we had toward her for letting him raise all this hell around us. She didn't have much of a solution for my sisters except to tell them to try and understand his behavior because that was their father. For me, she said I shouldn't be affected at all because he wasn't my dad. But, that was just it; she was trying to make me have respect for someone I didn't have to have respect for especially because of his actions.

I remember when I was three years old and I went into her room while she was sleeping. He was there, and he was up. When he saw me, he pushed me out of her room telling me to go back to my room. Ever since then, my respect for him had been out the window. I knew she knew damn well that this affected us; she just didn't want to take responsibility because it would make her seem like a bad person. She also wouldn't dare admit that I was right about anything. She always hated how much of a relationship I had with God but held no punches when it came to how she affected my life. She would be so quick to call me evil.

Anyway, at this meeting, he sat there and told us that my mom was the reason he was drinking and revealed to us the kinds of drugs he was doing. He tried so hard to get us to hate her for something we witnessed him doing. My sisters were in shock at how childish he was and clearly not willing to take any responsibility. I spoke up. I knew a thing, or two about depression and I just went ahead and said that's why he did the things he did.

"If she triggers you to drink, why be around her, why not free yourself?" I said.

"Because I want my family," he said.

Sady got so mad at that she lashed out and told him how much of a family we weren't. We were all stunned at that answer. Aheem yelled at Sady for speaking her truth, and she just went upstairs. I felt the urge to stick up for her. I calmed myself and I just simply said, "If you really care about your family then you would get some help. It's been twenty years, and you haven't changed a bit, we are honestly wondering why our mom even deals with you."

He just continued to be in denial that he had a problem, and like I expected, the conversation was pointless. Shortly after, he got so fucked up that he spat on my mom one morning, and as she began to retaliate, he threw toilet bowl water on her. No telling if there was anything in it or not. After she took him back for that, I was completely done with the both of them. All I cared about were my sisters. I made sure to tell her how stupid I thought she was for taking him back after all that. She felt that because he had "moved out" but was still here every day that she had control over the situation. I told her I could never be like her and her response was, "You're right. If you were like me, you'd know how to keep one man."

That was only the beginning of my stresses. What put the icing on the cake was one long day working both of my jobs, and I was the only one working my second job on a very busy day. On top of being physically tired and emotionally drained, this customer- who was not allowed to be in the store because of stealing- walked in. I politely asked her if she would remove herself because of reasons she was aware of. She didn't like how demanding I sounded and decided to come behind the counter and mush me. Needless to say, I lost my mind. It resulted in me losing that job. I looked at it as a blessing though. That was one less thing I had to stress about.

CHAPTER SIX

The Ripple Effect

The Ripple Effect
The ripple effect theory is a situation in which, like
ripples expand across the water when an object is
dropped into it, an effect from an initial state can be
followed outwards incrementally.

As hard as it was to forgive, I understood the importance of it all. If we don't forgive, we put an expectation on the person who hurt us to do something they do not choose to do, whether it's a confession or something as simple as an acknowledgment. Our hope for that makes us dependent on that person, thinking if we'd get that apology we will be happy. We hand them our power and become "tied" to them. Sometimes, you have to let people realize that they are the problem. Once we get into our system that vengeance belongs to God, then we can be mindful of the things we respond to and are consumed by. God will indeed take care of the problem the way he sees fit. But, until then, take your power back, free yourself and forgive. You will be able to live in your truth and receive blessings.

I was able to finally live in my truth unapologetically. The first person I forgave was my mother. Understanding forgiveness and accepting her for who she was made it easy. I started by taking some responsibility. I never told her what went on at my grandmother's house when she wasn't there, but I expected her just to know. When I had an abortion, her response to me wasn't very comforting, and I resented her for dealing with Aheem for so many years. I reacted to her in what she would call "evil ways" out of frustration of her lack of understanding of how these things affected me. I didn't have control over her actions, but I did have control over mine. Unfortunately, I fell into a deep depression which dictated how I maneuvered. I realized that she was only doing what she was taught to do. How could I really blame her? She never had a father present to show her how a man should treat her, so she was loving in the only way she knew how. She accepted certain behaviors because that's what love looked like to her.

Her lack of compassion came from her own abuse that never got any attention, so anything I was going through seemed dramatic to her and like the common black household, there are no such things as mental health issues. We were taught to get over our problems or be called straight up crazy. This dates back to the beginning of oppression to my mother, to her mother, and the mother before that and so on, and so forth. That first time my ancestor had to watch her children being taken away from her, then being told to deal with it, a behavior was taught. That first time my ancestor got raped by her slave master and had to just deal with it, a behavior was taught. Strength turned into bitterness and resentment toward the whole- hence, the "angry black woman." We were taught from that point on to only depend on ourselves for everything- emotionally too.

I learned to be content with the fact that I can break that cycle and pass my wisdom down to my offspring. I forgave the men that hurt me. I took responsibility for the fact that I knew these men were emotionally unavailable. I let the longing to be loved and protected force me to accept and adapt to someone else's version of happiness. Something like how my mom did. I thought that if I was everything they ever dreamt of, it would work in my favor. I confused my ability to see the king and queen in people for love. I know now that you can't love someone into loving you. I wasn't happy unless I was being myself. I knew that true love would not compromise me being anything less than myself. I used to think it was me. There must have been something about me that couldn't keep a man. It tore at my insecurities, and every time I met someone new, I changed something else that I loved about me to please them. I never really loved them. I just told myself that. I was in love with the idea, and I put expectations on them, hurting myself in the end.

My relationship with God taught me how to love unconditionally because that's how God loved me. No matter what I wore, how my hair was, or what I liked to do, nothing separated me from His love. I'm not excepting anything less because of that. I know whoever my true love is will choose me. What I know for sure and what I have learned from these men who are now happily in relationships is that a man is not gonna settle down until he is emotionally ready with whoever he picks. It doesn't matter how cute you are, how nice your body is, how much money you have, or how intellectual or smart you are, he has to be ready. Period. We, as women, think because we are so amazing a man should stop his biological clock and be ready for us. When he doesn't, we label him as a bad man. We rarely check ourselves and the intent behind why we want a man to love us so much. We may come to find that we aren't ready. Until you appreciate being alone, you'll never know if you're choosing someone out of love or loneliness. I can safely say that was my case.

I forgave every female I called my best friend. Not only did expectation ruin our friendships, but so did depression. I expected each one of them to have an unwavering amount of respect and love for me no matter how I acted. I realized that those were godly expectations. I take responsibility for putting that much pressure on them, whether they felt pressured or not. They too had an expectation for me that I could not fulfill due to depression and the need for me to depersonalize. I blamed them for their misunderstanding. They misunderstood how depression affected relationships and misunderstood the need for me to be free.

I wanted everybody I chose to be in my life as a scapegoat. I wanted equally-yoked friendships. I wanted them to understand how much my desire to live decreased as I poured and poured so much of me out without getting filled back up. I just got to a point where being mindful of everyone else's situation but mine was me not being fair to myself. I forgave my so-called girlfriends as well. I realized that I have to be okay with people's perception of me- even if they are wrong. I had to understand that how they viewed me had nothing to do with me but the version of me they chose to see made them feel comfortable. The light they saw in me was a threat. Little did they know I couldn't even see that in myself. People judge you negatively because of their own insecurities. When someone is secure in themselves, they don't care about how you live your life and aren't threatened by the greatness they see in you.

I didn't get to finish the third section of my vision board in Ohio because I still wasn't sure of anything other than the relationship between me and my mother was generational. When I got home, I felt like a big weight was lifted off my shoulders. For the rest of the summer, I got up every single day and walked 2 miles, straight shot, in my neighborhood. No, I didn't have any friends besides Boss and Thomas, and I was single. I was finally loving on myself, talking to God, listening to my old-lady music, meditating with my crystals, and blowing my trees in the wild just like I liked it.

I came home and wrote every day after walking, turning my thoughts into poetry. I even started putting some words together with a beat I made on my guitar. One day I wrote about how happy I was when I was living in my truth, but I still wasn't comfortable. I wasn't comfortable because the world around me wasn't living in theirs, which in turn made living in mine uncomfortable. The world encourages you to live in your truth, but then turns around and judges you. They don't understand that your soul is free because of truth. My body was still trapped in a prison because of the minds of other people. Then that's when it clicked- the last section of my vision board.

I remember it like it was yesterday, I came into my own sense of wokeness when I began to really think about my mental health. It made me think about other people's mental health—Uncle Norm's, my mom's, Aheem's. They all had been badly hurt before, and no one was there to help them.

In turn, much like myself, they had to learn to deal with that hurt on their own and ended up being an abuser themselves. I didn't excuse Uncle Norm's or Aheem's behavior because they still needed to take responsibility and get help. The saying, 'hurt people hurt people' came to mind and I changed the third section title on my vision board to that saying. I dug a little deeper. I can trace the hurt people 'hurt people' thing back from generations and generations of families teaching their children things they've learned from the generation before them. Somewhere along the line though there was a cutoff. Where did the hurt begin?

People from my cultural background can only date our history back to slavery times. Any time before then, was taken from us. We didn't get to have our family traditions passed down to us or any other knowledge of how our culture started civilization. All they gave us was the Prince of Egypt. But why, what's the psyche behind the person who decided to oppress a whole race of people? If we all have the same basic emotion, how were they able to keep oppression going for so many years? What if I told you we ALL suffer from oppression- black and white. It took me to have white friends to safely come to that conclusion. One of my good white friends actually admitted to me that she couldn't believe she had more in common with me than she did her other white friends when I told her about my life story. I decided to explore that a little. I dug a little bit deeper. What I do know from places other than school was that black and white people lived in their own native lands. Copper-colored people lived more civilized- like the kingdoms of Egypt, and ivory-colored people lived life like Vikings. Copper-colored people, who already were native to what we now call America were trading with Egyptians and other African countries. A group of copper-colored people called the Moors, was all about unity; they taught ivory- colored people about civilization, from the basics of science right down to how to have proper hygiene. Ivory- colored people started creating their own royal kingdoms, and so on, and so forth. The oppressed people from ivory civilizations rebelled and migrated to America. They mastered the hand-shake and a smile to the natives of America who were copper- colored.

Fast-forward to present day situations. The insecurities, jealousy, and absence of self-love from a group of people birthed oppression. Hurt people started hurting people. History was rewritten to favor the ivory being. Of course, oppressors never told their own people the real reason why they sought out vengeance, so instead, racism was beginning to be taught. Ivory people were being taught from birth to be afraid of copper-colored people for reasons that couldn't be explained. They were taught that they were better than copper- colored people and copper-colored people were made evil and were made slaves. They turned around and made copper-colored people raise their children, drink their breast milk and cook their meals. When the snatching of the babies began, the ivory women were confused as to why copper women would cry, because they were told that copper women had no emotion.

Meanwhile, our history, traditions, and culture were being snatched by the people who knew exactly what was going on. Copper-colored families started teaching their children to hold all of their emotions in because they would be penalized for it. Fast forward a little bit more to copper colored people being told that they were stupid and couldn't read by the ignorance of brainwashed ivory people. What they didn't realize was that we knew how to read, just not in the English language. So, when we were taught to read the English language and started speaking Ebonics, ivory people were confused by how quick and innovative copper-colored people were. We used hair braiding and astrology as a way to communicate the paths to freedom to each other; ivory people were confused because of what they were told. Once they realized that they were lied to, some chose to stay narcissistic, and others were more susceptible to realizing we are all human. The world started to change. The damage was done and continues to this day because copper-colored people are unaware of where we came from and the innate innovation we possess, out of fear of narcissists thinking that we indeed are better.

Oppression continues because of the fear from insecure narcissists who won't accept that they too have been lied to and we are all the same, birthing a contradictory law and school system keeping the oppressed in the same state and using false education as a way to make it in America. They used original African religion, flipped so it would glorify ivory background as a solution to our problems. In actuality, all the masses suffer from some type of mental disorder- whether it's narcissistic personality disorder or post-traumatic stress. How do I know? Because we all live life off of the mind-state of man, and not what God actually says. Jails are filled with copper-colored people- then they ask for money to be released. The irony of it all is that melanin is made up of the same properties of a diamond and cannot be duplicated, yet copper-colored people are the majority of the prison. We also supposed to be a Christian- based country, but the law of God says thou shall not kill; therefore, it cannot be justified, but the system bends that law and caters to ivory-colored people.

The more aware people became about the truth, the more laws, and rules of living catered to ivory-colored people. All the while telling us that we are finally "free" and "giving" us jobs and opportunities- that shouldn't have been exempt from us in the first place- because we built the joint. We believed that lie and started to be consumed by possessions. Possessions started distracting us from realizing the fact that the more knowledge of self we started to get and the more knowledge of truth started circulating, ivory people were protecting themselves by generational wealth and laws that cater to them.

I suddenly wanted to become an activist, an activist for truth, an activist to make mental health awareness a norm. The deprivation from the truth is stopping the world from gaining the knowledge that may help save the human race. What really matters is the betterment of the entire human race. When we work together, we may be surprised how much things about life itself we learn.

As I emerge into my supernatural rights, magically and divine,
my lights started to shine, understanding God is perfect with his time.
In the blue of evening, I am the midnight sun, night winds fall whispering well done.
When I was a sheep, there awaited the wolf to eat me whole, now behold the pretty soul.
Pretty soul, rose gold, beauty bold, story now told.
Pretty soul, evergreen, kind and keen like a daydream.
Pretty soul, pure and true, oh how it comforts you in secret rendezvous.
Complex like something Beethoven composed,
Smooth like honeydew, my spirit coos the fifth symphony "dun dun dun dun,"
I cue him every time I win.
Majestic like an Amerigo masterpiece, I only answer to your majesty.
Oh, barre Queen Sheba, something like Nefertiti,
These are the makings of me.
- Marnique Rogers

www.ingramcontent.com/pod-product-compliance
Lightning Source LLC
Chambersburg PA
CBHW060017100426
42740CB00010B/1510